The Law,
The Grace, The Love,
&
The Truth

The Law,
The Grace, The Love,
&
The Truth

Brandy Bennitt and Ian Mussman

YogiMind Publishing
Santa Barbara

Queries regarding rights and permission should be addressed to:
YogiMind Publishing
5142 Hollister Ave, #179
Santa Barbara, CA 93111
www.yogimind.com

Manufactured in the United States of America

ISBN: 9781449909895

*... I asked for all things, that I might enjoy life
I was given life that I might enjoy all things
I got nothing I asked for, but everything I had hoped for...*

-Unknown Confederate Soldier

Contents

Acknowledgements

There are many people in this dimension and beyond without whom this book would never have been written. We are eternally grateful to Rabbi Shimon bar Yochai, author of the Zohar ("The Book of Splendor") for his inspired wisdom, Isaac Luria (a.k.a. "The Ari"), Moses, Abraham and Joseph, as well as Jesus and Therese of Lisieux for spreading their light in this world and being universal guides to us all.

We also thank our personal divine guides as well as our spiritual teachers – Joel Goldsmith for Brandy, Paramhansa Yogananda and the teachers of his lineage as well as Rav Berg of the Kabbalah Center and Dr. David Hawkins for Ian.

We offer additional gratitude to Ammaji for her inspirational example, Brandy's beloved Auntie Loren for introducing her and Ian, Chitra Rao for helping Brandy to crush her ego, JJ Yoshihara for his energy and enthusiasm about the project, and Pace Lithographers for getting the book into print.

Preface

This book is based entirely upon research we conducted over the past 12 years using Biofeedback Resonance Testing and client case studies. Since many people are unfamiliar with how this sort of testing works, we offer a brief explanation here.

Biofeedback Resonance Testing is a form of testing based on the same principles as kinesiology testing in use today by many holistic practitioners. The core operating principle is that the physical body acts as a conductor for truth, and becomes strong in response to a statement of truth and weak in response to a false statement. Practitioners often use this method by asking a client to "resist" in response to a statement, and then pressing down on the client's outstretched arm (deltoid muscle) to see if the arm is strong or weak. Strength indicates truth, while weakness indicates falsity. Although this method is simple, it takes practice and experience to learn to phrase questions correctly and it is important that the questions asked not be egoistic or self-serving in nature, as that will decrease or nullify the accuracy of the response.

In Biofeedback Resonance testing, the same sort of test as described above is performed more quickly by using computerized biofeedback equipment and measuring the galvanic skin response on various acupuncture points. The client holds a ground in one hand and a mild electrical current is conducted through the client's body through acupuncture points on the other hand, creating a circuit. Resistance by the body signifies a yes answer while lack of resistance signifies a no answer. Holistic health care practitioners usually use this method to determine resonance between a client and a particular treatment or remedy, but any yes/no question can receive an answer using this technique; its usefulness is not limited in any way by the knowledge of the practitioner or the subject, nor does the question necessarily need to pertain to the subject. The difference in accuracy between one practitioner and another using this method is determined by their level of skill and by the level of consciousness of the practitioner. The accuracy of the testing improves as the personality-based emotional attachment to the outcome diminishes.

For a more thorough explanation of the principles at work in this sort of testing we recommend the reader investigate Dr. David R. Hawkins' *Power vs. Force,* or any of his other wonderful works.

Introduction

Guy Levoyer was a gentle man with a warm smile and an air of modesty. In a photograph taken of him just a few months prior to his death he is wearing glasses but you can still see the sparkle of his eyes even behind their thick lenses. He looks very French, as he was, and the feeling one gets from his smile and humble posture is that this is a man who would be prone to sweet interactions with everyone, from his family members to harried shopkeepers to cranky bureaucrats.

In late spring of 2008 we received the unexpected news that Ian's uncle Guy had passed away in Paris. Ian, who was raised there, although he had left at the age of 19 to move to the U.S., was close with his mother's family in France. Guy, his mother's brother, had been a favorite of his, and Ian had hoped to visit him that spring, but circumstances had delayed the trip. When he learned of Guy's death, his grief was deep, not only for the loss of his beloved uncle, but for the lesson that Guy's life appeared to signify, which can be expressed simply: for some people, life is cruel, and then they die. The terrible, incomprehensible fact of Guy's life that gave Ian such cognitive discomfort was that right when Guy's circumstances were about to finally get better, he died. It would be impossible to understand Ian's grief and confusion over this without understanding a bit of Guy's history.

The fascinating thing about Guy's life is that it seemed so dreadful to an outside observer. He was born in pre-World War II France. As an infant, he had a reaction to his immunizations and almost died. He also developed severe, chronic dermatitis that plagued him for the rest of his life, giving rise to a permanent feeling of inferiority and physical discomfort.

In 1940, when he was four years old, France was invaded by Germany. For the next five years there was very little food or heating oil available, and so he (like so many European children of the time), suffered from hunger and deprivation. His father was an emotionally distant and abusive alcoholic who eventually left the family and later died of liver cirrhosis.

He married at age twenty-four, and almost died on his wedding day from anaphylactic shock from an allergic reaction to the coconut in the wedding cake. His wife had a long-term affair with his sister's husband, a man who also happened to be his boss. After he divorced her and resigned from his position, she continued as his brother-in-law's mistress for twenty years.

A couple of years after his divorce he was involved in a severe car accident. Later, he started his own plumbing business but he became unable to continue in that profession due to a chronic allergic skin reaction to the chemicals he used.

He experienced a second car accident a few years after his business failed. He then married a very jealous and controlling woman who made his life miserable until she ultimately left him.

In his late fifties, he was laid off from his long-term position in the nuclear industry. After a long period of unemployment he eventually became a bar manager in Normandy. One night he was caught in a bar brawl with a gang of bikers. He was beaten up, the bar was destroyed, and Guy had to be hospitalized not only for his physical injuries but also for the associated emotional breakdown. This led to a severe, almost fatal allergic reaction that kept him hospitalized for weeks.

When he was finally released from the hospital, he found himself, in his early sixties, unemployed and penniless. He was forced to move in with his domineering mother in the tiny apartment where he had grown up. Eventually, his elderly mother became ill and he took care of her for the rest of her (and as it turned out, his) life. For twelve long years, it was just the two of them in the small apartment. He was afraid she would die if he left her side, so he chose to become a shut-in. When his mother finally passed on, he spent several months cleaning out the apartment and settling her affairs, and then Guy died.

What should have happened instead was simple: now that Guy was finally free of his caretaking responsibilities for his mother, he would move to the South of France to live out the rest of his life with his sister. The two close (and single) siblings would care for one another in their golden years in the beautiful rosy light of Provence, drinking wine, discussing philosophy, and living simple lives in the small beautiful village where his sister resides.

The fact that this happy ending to such a hard life was denied to Guy was the main source of Ian's consternation over the age-old question about the meaning of life. It was clear that Guy suffered a great deal throughout his life, and according to our sense of fairness, when one suffers, at least there should be a reward for the suffering. For Guy, this did not seem to be the case. Right when he should have received his reward, he died.

Perhaps you know someone like this, someone who just doesn't seem to get a break. We certainly know of other examples ourselves, and Guy is obviously not the only good person to experience brutally unfair conditions in life through what would appear to be no fault of his own. In considering Guy it seemed to us that in order to understand the meaning of our own lives, it was necessary to understand once and for all, why it is that bad things happen to good people.

Although we had both devoted our careers to understanding the human condition in terms of physical, emotional, and mental wellbeing, this was the first time we really began to ask questions that had a more philosophical, even metaphysical, basis. As we embarked upon our investigation, we had a lucky break. A tiny thread appeared that in time wove itself into a magnificent tapestry, and it was in this tapestry that we saw the image of a world that does run according to laws of truth and love, although most of us do not have the proper tools to discern it. That first thread came in the form of a question, as though a voice had whispered the suggestion into our ears:

"Is there a scale to tell if a person is driven more by fear or by love?"

The answer is yes.

This simple question, along with its equally simple answer, led immediately to a barrage of other questions. Of course, these led to answers that led to more questions, and the result of those is this book you hold in your hands.

Ultimately, what we were seeking to understand was how we could live happier, healthier lives full of positive circumstances instead of cruel or limiting conditions. The answers we received surprised us, but after consideration, we realized they resonated with us. As we began to use this theory with our clients, we started to see not only consistent patterns, but remarkable results as well.

We were led to look for divine love directly within the experiences that had previously seemed to derail all our happy plans and to understand that a true state of forgiveness occurs only when we finally and fully realize there was never anyone or anything to forgive, that every piece of our lives was there through our own highest intention, through the need and longing of our own soul. The theory that developed from all of this questioning and testing has completely revolutionized our worldview. Life makes sense now in a way it never did before, and the gratitude we hold for all the experiences of our lives, most especially the difficult trials, is overwhelming.

Through our research we have come to understand that it is precisely those challenging experiences that are responsible for allowing us to eventually achieve the state where our goals and dreams are realized, and they do so in a very direct, calibrated, predictable manner. Once we learn the pattern of how Life hurls us our challenges, we can learn not only to appreciate them, but also to overcome them and as a result, bypass our need for them.

There is indeed a simpler, less painful path, and our goal is to share that knowledge with as many people as possible.

The Law,
The Grace, The Love,
&
The Truth

I. The Ego

ONE

The State of Truth

We are a modest society in at least one regard: very few of us have devoted ourselves exclusively to the goal of attaining spiritual success. Let's face it, most of us feel that spiritual illumination is beyond our reach, so rather than seek such a lofty spiritual goal we settle for material comfort, professional achievement, financial stability, and satisfaction in our romantic and family lives. If you doubt the truth of this statement, take a visit to the self-help section of your local bookstore. You'll find the majority of the books there deal with at least one of these issues. Or better yet, try this exercise: grab a pen and write down the five biggest worries that have occupied your attention in the past week. If you are like the majority of people, at least one of those, and probably more than one, will conform to one of those five areas (health, career, money, family or relationships).

These are the main concerns of the majority of people in our society.

Now, there is nothing in this book that condemns those goals. On the contrary, they are very reasonable. What we are really saying is this: we want to enjoy our lives on this planet. Yet, something seems to be standing in the way for most of us. We set for ourselves what we think of as modest goals and yet despite this focus, we often find these seemingly simple things elude us, not due to our own lack of determination but due to outside circumstances that inflict their punishments upon us. Life, it seems, will not leave us alone long enough for us to pursue our simple objectives in peace, and as a result, we experience great suffering and frustration.

The question then arises: how can we achieve satisfaction in our lives if we are beset by challenges and tragedies that are apparently not our fault, and over which we seem to have no control? How can we focus on our goals if our spouse is suddenly taken from us by illness, or if our children get into trouble? How will we reach a state of happiness if conflicts not of our own making reach into our lives and take loved ones, or if traffic accidents, lawsuits, or bankruptcies disrupt our otherwise well-laid plans? It seems impossible to live a happy and fulfilled life when such seemingly random events are constantly occurring, or threatening to happen. Resigning ourselves to the truism, "Life isn't fair" doesn't bring us any closer to the peace, love, happiness and connection we seek.

Of course when tragedy strikes, most of us are plagued by the question, "Why is this happening to ME?" Even most religions and philosophies are unable to provide satisfactory answers to this question. The scriptures tell us there is a loving God that has not forgotten us. We often ask how this is possible. If we look at the suffering in the world, most of us would agree there does not seem to be any God around protecting human lives or livelihoods. How can we be calm when we feel constantly threatened and unprotected? How can we be loving and open when we have learned that to do so means to expose ourselves to possible hurt? And furthermore, *why would we want to?*

This purpose of this book is to give simple, straightforward answers to these questions. It is to explain the function of these tragic experiences, to give a satisfactory answer to the question of why we would want to open our hearts and to offer a precise and simple roadmap for bypassing the worst of the tragedies. Believe it or not, there is a clear and direct reason why we have terrible experiences, and there is also a way to transcend our need for them and transform our responses to them if and when they do come. There is also a compelling reason for why we would want to open our hearts to others, to care about the welfare of other human beings, to be our brother's keeper, and this book explains how doing so will directly influence our ability to meet our own personal goals.

One of the important things we have discovered is this: there is such a thing as a state of Truth, and more importantly, that state is the birthright of every human being. Every one of us is on the road there, whether we're aware of it or not. In fact, it is in this state that the goals mentioned above will finally and permanently be realized. But it is the state of Truth that we must seek first, not the goals themselves. Until we reach that state, any gains we might make on those goals will be washed away, or will fail to bring us genuine, complete fulfillment. This point cannot be overemphasized: *we must first seek a state of Truth*, for until we arrive there, everything else we may seem to gain will not bring us what we desire.

This state is the divine nature of every human being, and the inescapable purpose of our life here on earth is to achieve permanent consciousness of this state, not just as individuals, but also as a society. Amazingly, it exists within us already, yet we are unaware of it. We are blocked from realizing our true nature by the influence of our ego, and by the restriction of our hearts. Therefore, the road to this state is paved with the challenge of dropping our negativity and limited sense of self and opening our hearts to accommodate the infinite, boundless essence of our souls.

In this book, we refer to the first part of the process as *dropping the ego*, which brings us to a state of Grace, and the second part as *building soulfulness*, which brings us to a state of Love. When you combine a state of Grace with a state of Love, and go deeper into each, you achieve a state of Truth. When you are in a state of Truth, any goal you may set will be achieved gracefully, effortlessly and in perfect timing. This book is a precise and simple roadmap of the journey there, and the options and challenges you have along the way. Whether you know it or not, you are already on the road to Truth and you are already experiencing the challenges of that journey. This book is merely here to illuminate the meaning of those challenges so you may overcome them more easily, and perhaps bypass some of them entirely

TWO

What Is the Ego?

There are a number of definitions of ego, most famously that of Sigmund Freud. The ego as we define it in this book is significantly different from Freud's definition, which involves a complex interplay between the superego, ego, and id. Our ego is much simpler.

We define ego as the belief in a "self" separate and apart from every other "self." It is the dualistic belief in the "other," and as such, when a human being is acting from a place of ego, that human being is focused on struggling with forces he believes to be outside of himself.

The stronger a person's ego, the more tempted that person will be to place blame for her circumstances on external forces, whether those forces be socio-economical, political or simply other people. This person will be tempted to believe that these circumstances have power over her, and because of that belief, will engage in struggles against them. Plato described this struggle elegantly in his *Allegory of the Cave[1]:* it is a fight with shadows we believe are real.

The lower the influence of an individual's ego, the less tempted that person is to place blame and engage in struggle with outer circumstances or other people, and the more inclined that person is to look inward, recognize that his inner state is the source of all circumstances in his experience, and actively engage in inner transformation.

The High Ego person is focused on outer circumstances such as financial, medical, and relational. He sees life as a struggle of "man against nature" or "woman against society," or some other universal struggle, pitting himself against all others (it may simply be "me against the world").

---

[1] For interested readers: *The Allegory of the Cave* is written as a fictional dialogue between Plato's teacher Socrates and Plato's brother Glaucon, at the beginning of Book VII of Plato's *Republic* (514a-520a).

In contrast, the low-ego person is led to engage in active inner transformation. When outer circumstances do not measure up to his expectations, the low-ego person is able to turn within, and in the quietness of his soul, reflect on how this outer circumstance really reflects what is going on within himself. He can then take action based on the insight that he receives, inwardly transforming to shift the outer picture.

The high-ego person is compelled to react to circumstances and events. The low-ego person is able to simply respond. Even more importantly, where the high-ego person sees tragedy, the low-ego person sees an opportunity for further growth and love. Let this not be forgotten: to a low-ego person, circumstances are never tragic; they are simply circumstances, the stuff of which life is made. Although anger and fear may still arise in a low-ego person, he or she is able to release the emotion and stay in a centered state regardless of what occurs.

Of course, there are not just high-ego people and low-ego people. There is an entire continuum of different ego zones, and so we have come up with an Ego Power scale that is measured from 0% to 100%. The percentages represent the amount of time that a person is acting and thinking through the perspective of the ego, rather than through the ego-less perspective of the soul. So, for example, a 100% ego person would be completely dominated by the egoic perspective, one hundred percent of the time, and a 0% ego person is completely free from the ego. A person at 50% ego is dominated by her ego 50% of the time. That may sound like a lot, but actually, the majority of people rate higher than that.

The name for the state of low ego (below 45%) is a *state of Grace.* The ego is synonymous with fear, selfishness, shame, guilt, hatred, envy, separation, and all other forms of negativity, and the way to a state of Grace is to reduce one's ego to the lowest level possible. There are specific ways to do this, and they are outlined in this book. Before we go on to examine how to lower the ego, however, let's spend a little time explaining why you would want to. We'll start with exploring what life is like when we are dominated by our ego and how it changes when we lower the ego.

THREE

The Law

Most of humanity is living in a state of survival where they are completely bound by the Law of Punishment and Reward, also known as the Law of Cause and Effect or the Law of Karma. This Law is simple: everything that occurs has an equal and opposite reaction. When we live under this Law, we are not free – we are subject to the actions of others, or to the effect of world conditions. Most importantly, this Law demands that the Universe give us an equal and opposite reaction to our own ego-based actions and beliefs, and we are therefore continually assaulted by the returning waves of our own negativity. The result of this Law is that most of humanity lives in the midst of chaos, plagued by unexpected disasters and uncertainty about the future. We live lives controlled by fear and distrust, lack and unhappiness. On a global level, there are wars, human rights violations, famines, plagues and natural disasters. We react to these negative conditions with more negativity; when we are attacked, we refuse to forgive. When we suffer deprivation or disaster, we look out for ourselves above all others. Whether it is for our family, our tribe, our political faction or our country, we protect our own first. When we meet with injustice, we perpetuate it upon others. This is the essence of life lived under the Law. Of course people living under the Law doubt the existence of a Divine Order, for when we look at life under the Law it appears merciless, cruel and unforgiving.

When we are ruled by the ego, we are living under the Law. When we drop the ego, we are living under Grace, because Grace is what is left when the Ego is gone. Again, this is a continuum: we enter a state of Grace as our ego drops below 45% (at which point we are no longer controlled by our ego the majority of the time but instead harmoniously directed by our soul) but this is not the end of the journey. The lower our ego goes, the more Grace becomes available to us, and the more we find our lives governed and supported by Grace.

FOUR

The State of Grace

In the state of Grace, we generally live lives of integrity and reason. We are cognizant of other beings and how our words and actions affect them, and we usually make an earnest effort to be kind and thoughtful towards others. At this point, the majority of our struggles are internal, and we are aware of them as challenges to overcome our own negativity and resistance. Although difficult or trying circumstances may still surface in our life's journey, we no longer react to such things with the fear and anxiety we used to. Somehow, we know that even if things don't go the way we want them to, we'll be all right anyway. This is a significant shift in our human experience.

The lower we drop our egos in a state of Grace, the more we are able to truly surrender to the flow of our lives. As we go further into this state, we begin to have the capacity to overcome fear and anxiety and exist in trust and certainty. An individual deep in this state (in the low, low ego zone) no longer feels overwhelmed by fears over outer circumstances and how they may affect her. When she is confronted with challenging circumstances, she is able to respond, rather than react. This person does not see life as a battle against external forces but as an inner struggle against fear, negativity and selfishness. The lower her ego drops, the more this is true for her.

This state of Grace is impossible to achieve if we are ruled by our ego, for the ego tells us to fight the flow of life, not surrender to it. The ego threatens us with fearful images of the future and holds us in bondage to our belief in our victimization. When we have a high ego, we feel that if we were to let go of it, we would lose our identity completely. This is an illusion the ego creates to trick us into perpetuating its existence. This is why we want to drop it, because our ego is what prevents us from living in the harmonious flow of Life. When we are dominated by the ego, we are not in a state of Grace – we are living under the Law of Cause and Effect.

Now that we understand what the ego is, and what the consequences are for living a life dominated by ego, it is easy to see why we would want to drop it. The next question, of course, is *how*? To understand that, we must first understand the different *levels* of ego, and the difference between *passive* ego dropping and *active* ego dropping.

A Side Note About Death

Although a belief in reincarnation is not necessary in order to be interested in this book or the theory it presents, it certainly helps. If you believe that this is your only lifetime and there never was another one before this one, and there won't be any more after this one, it doesn't mean you can't put this theory into practice. It just means that you are going to have to work hard to lower your ego this time around and not wait until a future lifetime to do so. That being said, following is a description of what our research has led us to conclude about life and death.

There will never be a world without death any more than there will be a world without seasons. Just as winter must surely and necessarily come, death and endings come to all of us, and to every civilization. Permanence is not a measure of importance, for all things are ultimately temporal, even the mountains and the seas. That this is a necessary condition and not simply an inconvenience or a sorrow is important to remember; otherwise we will mourn unnecessarily when a flower dies, forgetting that spring must end in order for summer to begin. Death and rebirth are inextricably linked together, of equal importance, and must be treated with equal reverence.

We are in our truest essence infinite beings, without ending or beginning. In this context, death is not a finality, it is merely the conclusion to one chapter of our existence - and a very necessary one, for it is only by closing one chapter that we may start a new one. Our theory examines the human condition on both a personal, individual level and on a wider, group level in the context of the entire history of humankind, not in the limited terms of our own present lifetimes. As we dig deeper, it becomes increasingly apparent that we are all in the middle of our endless stories, and for every ending a new beginning awaits us.

The important thing to remember about death in reference to the ego is that with one exception, we are always re-born with the same ego score with which we died in our previous lifetime. Thus, the ego lowering process continues uninterrupted throughout different incarnations for each of us. The exception to this rule relates to the very first level of ego: New Souls.

FIVE

The Five Levels of Ego

Although the ego power scale represents a complete continuum from 100% to 0%, there are five different levels within that continuum. When an individual drops from one level to another – even though at times that means dropping just one point – there is a significant shift in his life experience.

The first level is the highest level, and it includes only one level of ego: 100%. This is the state in which each of us lives our very first lifetime as a human being, thus we also refer to 100% ego individuals as "New Souls." People who are at 100% feel the pull of their ego so strongly it is almost impossible for them to deny it or overcome it. The thought of true surrender is almost abhorrent to them because the ego is so strong it overpowers all else. New souls generally focus completely on the outer circumstances of their lives, and engage in struggle against those circumstances, rather than focusing on inner transformation. This lifetime is not dedicated to overcoming the ego. Rather, it is more about just getting comfortable being a human being and experiencing as much as possible of what this world has to offer.

Although the lives and actions of New Souls are generally characterized by conflict and competition, they are among the greatest helpers to the rest of us because it is they who help everyone else to lower their egos. New Souls tend to draw the negativity out of other people so that they can recognize and release it. This is both incredibly frustrating and a truly wonderful gift.

Engagement with a New Soul will never be a conflict-free enterprise, but it will offer a prime opportunity for the engager to destroy or reduce his ego in some way, through one or more of many specifically identified negative experiences.

Remember, we were all New Souls once, and some of us are currently in this state. Although there are many ways a soul can reduce the power and control of the ego, none of them apply to a New

Soul except for the last: death. Upon death, the ego drops to 99%, which is where the soul is re-born. At this point, the soul enters what we refer to as the "High Ego" stage.

This is the second stage of Ego, and the soul moves out of this stage when it has successfully reduced the ego to below 75%. It is here, in this second stage, that the soul can now begin to actively (or passively, as you shall see) drop the ego.

The third stage, which we refer to as the "Medium Ego" stage, starts at 74% and lasts until the individual lowers the ego below 45%.

The fourth stage, which we refer to as the "Low Ego" stage, begins at 44% and continues down to 1%. However, even once the individual has accomplished this lowering of the ego, he must remain on guard: the ego can always rise again. Vigilance is still required.

The fifth and final stage is when the ego is fully released, and the individual is free from the grip of the ego forever (0%). This state is beyond our current understanding, but we are aware that it exists. For the practical purposes of this book, we will confine ourselves to dealing only with the first four stages of ego.

SIX

The High Ego Zone: 99% to 75%

For every stage except the "New Soul" stage there is a list of ways through which the individual may lower his or her ego. You will notice that the higher the ego, the more challenges come to the individual in the form of imposed circumstances, while the lower the ego, the more challenges are of inner transformation. Let us begin at the "High Ego Zone" and discuss the different options Life gives us to lower our egos (please see the list on the next page)

Not a pretty list, is it? Up to now you may have been excited to discover how you can drop your ego. At this point, you may be tempted to close this book and say, "No thank you, I don't need to read about imprisonment or dismemberment." We urge you to read on. There is more, and the news does get better.

High Ego Zone Challenges

1. Suffering

2. Loss

3. Failure

4. Submission

5. Humiliation

6. Violence

7. Incapacitation

8. Dependency

9. Involuntary Caretaking

10. Domination (for females) / Emasculation (for males)

11. Divorce

12. Exile / Banishment

13. Financial Ruin

14. Accidents

15. Legal Trials

16. Imprisonment

17. Sexual Violation

18. Dismemberment

19. Untimely Death

20. Torture

21. Murder / Execution

There will be a whole chapter on the subject of *passive* ego lowering versus *active* ego lowering. For now, let us reassure you the list above is not the only way to lower your ego – it is simply the list of the ways in which most people unconsciously (or, as we like to term it, *passively*) lower their own egos. Rest assured that none of the above experiences are absolutely necessary for anyone. However, all of us have at least some of those experiences anyway, and there is a reason for that: it is because we are not aware there is another way to lower our egos. We therefore attract challenging circumstances into our lives. Through these we experience great suffering and as a result, we overcome our own inner resistance to change and ultimately release our egos little by little.

In other words, while that list of experiences is not necessary to lower our egos, it is the default way in which most of us unconsciously do so. We will address the uncommon, faster, *active* way to lower our egos in a later chapter. Our goal now is to help you gain an understanding of your own past experiences and what they brought to you as we examine specific examples of passive ego lowering through our relevant case studies.

As you examine the list of High Ego Zone Challenges, you may notice a certain order to the potential ego lowering events on the list. If you look closely, it is apparent that Life has much more rational logic in the trials and challenges it gives us than most of us give it credit for. Much like a loving parent trying to teach a child responsibility, each time we resist meeting the challenge before us (and the challenge is always the same: to let go of our ego) Life sends us a progressively more powerful challenge to overcome our resistance.

So, for example, if we do not give up our ego through an accident, we may find ourselves confronted by a legal trial. If we continue to cling to self-righteousness through our trial, we may find ourselves confronted subsequently by imprisonment, and so forth. Or perhaps we give up a little bit of our ego at each of these junctures but not the whole thing (to give up the entire ego, all at once, is a rare occurrence, but we have seen examples of individuals who dropped 40 points in a single moment). Until we completely surrender to the flow of our lives, Life will continue to push us to give up more of our ego (which is what stands in the way of the flow of our lives).

Now that you understand the theory of how this works, let's look at some specific examples. As it happens, examples of ego lowering are all around us – in our own lives, in our friends' lives, and even in the lives of fictional characters. In fact, our first case study is a fictional, yet nevertheless realistic, example. We chose this one because it is a well-known story, and because the story accurately portrays a character going through the process of ego lowering. Fiction or not, archetypes hold true, and this is precisely what gives certain stories such widespread, popular appeal: our subconscious recognizes the truth embedded within the archetypes the characters represent and is therefore able to relate to their stories.

Thus, without further ado, we give you... *Batman*. This case study is drawn from the extremely well written narrative for the movie, *Batman Begins*[2], and its sequel, *The Dark Knight*[3]

---

[2] Nolan, C. (Director), Franco, L., (Producer), & Kane, B., Goyer, D., Nolan, C. (Writers). (2005). *Batman Begins* [Theatrical], United States: Warner Bros. Pictures.

[3] Nolan, C. (Director), de la Noy, K. (Producer), & Nolan, J., Nolan, C., Goyer, D., Kane, B. (Writers). (2008), *The Dark Knight* [theatrical], United States: Warner Bros. Pictures.

Notes from the files of an Ego investigation
Subject: Bruce Wayne, aka "Batman"

Event: Birth
Ego Score: 97
STATUS: HIGH EGO

Event: Falls down a well into a cave
Suffering: Accident, humiliation, incapacitation
Ego points: -12
Ego score: 85
STATUS: HIGH EGO

Event: Parents murdered
Suffering: Untimely death of loved ones, loss
Ego Points: -15
Ego Score: 70
STATUS: MEDIUM EGO

Event: Denied the opportunity to avenge his parents' death, subsequent scuffle with thugs
Suffering: Failure, humiliation, violence, domination

Ego points: -5
Ego score: 65
STATUS: MEDIUM EGO

Event: Leaves home to go abroad and make his way through the underworld
Suffering: Exile, violence
Ego Points: -5
Ego Score: 60
STATUS: MEDIUM EGO

Event: Arrested and thrown into a Chinese prison camp
Suffering: Imprisonment, violence
Ego Points: -10
Ego Score: 50
STATUS: MEDIUM EGO

Event: As a result of a fight, he is put into solitary confinement within the prison camp.
Suffering: Imprisonment, violence, banishment
Ego Points: -6
Ego Score: 44
STATUS: LOW EGO

At this point, the subject had achieved the necessary score to no longer require passive suffering in order to reduce his ego. As a result, he was immediately released from the prison camp.

Event: Trained as a ninja
Ego Clearing: Self-discipline, non-reactivity, patience, taking full responsibility, humility, surrender
Ego Points: -10
Ego Score: 35
STATUS: VERY LOW EGO

The first thing you may notice from this case study is that for each of these events, not only were there points deducted from the ego, there was a specific number of points. We'll get to the explanation of this a little later. For now, let's examine the most important parts of this case study.

Bruce was born with a rather high ego, 97%. This put him deep into the High Ego zone from the very beginning of his life. Of course, a child born to billionaire, philanthropist parents would have relatively few opportunities for ego reduction if he also had a happy childhood. But Bruce didn't. His first terrifying experience in the bat cave that traumatized him, combined with an injured leg, did a lot to lower his ego, and the brutal murder of his parents brought him completely below the High Ego Zone and into the Medium Ego Zone.

You may have noticed in your own life that when you go through periods of trial or suffering that you begin to feel lighter in a way, and perhaps less resistant to the challenges of life. We may think of this state as the result of emotional loss, and while that is true, it is also true that it is in this state that we find our ego substantially reduced. Unfortunately, it does not always remain so.

Back to our hero: when Bruce is denied the opportunity to avenge his parents' death, his ego drops even further, low enough for him to recognize the wisdom of putting into action a very courageous plan. He decides to leave home and make his way in the world, not as the billionaire that he is, but as a member of the underworld. He experiences hunger and lack of shelter and what it is like not only to be a thief but also to be arrested as one. Interestingly, none of those things lower his ego until he is actually thrown into a Chinese prison camp. Perhaps this is because he knows that at any moment he could make one simple phone call and get out of any mess he is in – until his freedom is taken from him. At this point, he experiences another significant drop in his ego.

His last major drop comes at the point when he is thrown into solitary confinement. This one small thing drops him out of the Medium Ego Zone and into the Low Ego zone. Interestingly, and very consistent with this theory, he is immediately released. This fits: when an individual's ego drops below 45%, into the Low Ego Zone, there is no longer any need for him to have outer challenges imposed upon him to lower his ego. Now, he is in the Low Ego Zone, and in this zone, the optimal way to lower the ego further is through inner transformation. Therefore, typically when an individual moves into the Low Ego Zone, severe outer challenges tend to shift. Whether the outer condition persists or not, the individual's perspective on the condition is transformed, and he is not so tempted to struggle with it. His tendency now is stronger than ever to turn within and focus on inner transformation. This tendency is the pull of our own soul, seeking to fulfill its purpose here on Earth, but the tendency is blocked or masked by the ego when it is strong, because its messages pull us in the opposite direction.

It is common, however, for individuals to lower their egos to 44% and then stop, as any further ego reduction is a matter of choice, and depends entirely upon the individual's active commitment to inner transformation. Further ego reduction will help move the individual deeper into the state of Grace that we have already described, so there is substantial motivation to continue the journey – but the process can no longer proceed passively. In Bruce's case, he chose to train as a ninja, which involved a serious devotion to inner transformation. He chose to continue the ego-lowering journey.

Let us return now to Guy, and look at his life in the context of ego dropping, rather than the situational context. There are two important things that we learned when we looked at Guy's ego: at birth it was 99%, high up in the high ego zone, and by the time of his death, it was at 30, in the very low ego zone. This amounts to a rather incredible lifetime drop of almost 70 points.

It is this sort of example that makes it easier to believe that our souls experience multiple lifetimes. When he is re-born, he will have an ego of 30%, in a state of Grace. It should be a beautiful life next time around for Guy's soul.

Yet, this example brings to mind the question: does it need to be so miserable? It is probably safe to assume that everyone is interested in achieving a state of Grace. But most of us aren't brave enough (or to put it another way, crazy enough) to map out quite so horrible a life for ourselves in order to reach that place (not that Guy did it intentionally – he didn't. He just chose the passive road). Is it necessary to have a horrible, painful, dreadful life in order to lower our egos?

No, it is not. Actually, there is only one thing required to lower our ego: discipline, which is sometimes called spiritual will. If you know how to lower your own ego, you have a wonderful prospect of doing so without too much damage to your psyche – and doing it more quickly and less painfully. Again, this is called *active* ego lowering, and it will be discussed in detail in a future chapter. But first we must explain a few more things about dropping our ego passively so it is clear exactly how this works, and why passive ego lowering is such a long, drawn-out, and miserable process with serious emotional repercussions.

SEVEN

Ego Rising

Looking at Guy's life, we see that at several different junctures, he experienced painful circumstances that caused him to drop ego points, but then he regained them. This is precisely the pattern that the majority of us follow. We crush our egos, and then rebuild them. Destroy, rebuild. No wonder it takes so much pain and misery to overcome them for good!

But how does the ego go back up? This brings us to another important principle: ego lowering is an exact science. For every event on the ego lowering list, there is a specific, corresponding ego lowering score range. For instance, dismemberment can drop your score up to 15 ego points, and imprisonment can reduce your ego from 5-20 points, depending on how long the prison term is and whether you were innocent or guilty (See the chart on page 66 for detail of this).

Whenever you experience any one of the ego lowering events on the list, your ego immediately drops those points, right then and there. Then you go into what we call the **90-day deadline period**. Yes, this is starting to sound like a board game. Well, it only gets better.

Here is the rule: If, within ninety days after your ego is lowered, you still harbor resentment about the gift of the ego lowering experience, or if you believe yourself to be a victim of the experience – in other words, if you *reject* the gift of the experience – your ego goes back up. That's right – easy come (or really, not so easy), easy go.

If you break the 90-day rule and your ego score goes back up, you will still have the chance to redeem some of those lost points at a later date should you come to a realization of the gift of the experience – but you won't be able to redeem all of them. How many you can redeem is directly proportional to the depth of your gratitude for the experience.

If this is starting to sound arbitrary to you, that's understandable, but rest assured that it is not.

Sometimes it is difficult for us to believe that natural laws apply to the human condition just as surely as they apply to the natural world, yet this is indeed a natural law: ninety days is the length of a season. Ninety days is also the industry standard for new hires in business. Why ninety days? Well, ninety days appears to be the length of time we are given to capitalize on any opportunity. Like any farmer with his seeds will tell you, if you don't plant in the right season, the opportunity will pass you by. Granted, the opportunity will come around again the next year, but you'll have to wait for it until then. Likewise any Human Resources manager will tell you that it takes about ninety days to determine if a new hire is appropriate for his position. In other words, a new hire has ninety days to seize the opportunity the employment is offering to him. If the employee fails to do so, he will be let go.

What we are really talking about is a natural law that governs how long we have to seize and capitalize on an opportunity before the moment has passed, and that is precisely what an ego lowering event is – an opportunity. We can, through our own stubbornness and blindness, refuse the blessing of an ego lowering event, and if so, in ninety days our ego will go back to where it was before. Just like a gardener who didn't plant her seeds in time this year, there will be another opportunity later, but it won't happen right away. We just have to wait, and we'll never be able to move the clock backward and take back a chance that was missed.

There are specific actions and attitudes that cause us to refuse the opportunity of an ego lowering event and allow our ego to rise. In fact, our ego can go up at any time at all if we indulge in any one of these attitudes or practices. As you might expect, there is a list (see the next page).

Our research has shown us that these are life themes. In other words, although all of us have probably experienced each of these temptations grabbing hold of our psyches at different instances in our lives, we really only struggle with specific ones, and it's a continuous, ongoing life struggle. Some people only have one way their ego rises, others have two or three. To date, we have not seen anyone with more than three.

In Guy's case, although he was an alcoholic who eventually died of liver failure and septicemia

Ego Rising

1. Lack of discipline

2. Lack of love

3. Ingratitude

4. Feeling of Superiority

5. Desire for Power and Dominance

6. Anger and Resentment

7. Substance Abuse and Addiction

(blood poisoning), substance abuse was not what made his ego rise over and over again. What made his ego rise was anger, specifically anger at his brother-in-law/former boss and his first wife as well as other people in his life he felt had wronged him. Note that energetically the liver is where we hold and store anger. Because he was unable to let this anger go, his ego often rose again, which meant he had to repeat the process of lowering it many, many times through cycles of suffering. His plight calls to mind the myth of Prometheus, who grew back his liver daily only to have it eaten again and again by an implacable raptor.

Yes, it is possible to hold onto anger for a lifetime. From our experience with our clients, not only is it possible – it is common. Many people are surprised when they come to see us and discover that the anger charge they still hold from events in their childhood is at a full 100%. We are often unaware of what we are carrying around with us.

Guy is not alone among our case studies to experience ego rising as well as ego lowering. Let's go back to our first case study: Bruce Wayne. This time, instead of observing his ego steadily dropping, we observe it rising as well.

Although it took an enormous amount of suffering, discipline, and hard work for Bruce to lower his ego from 97% to 35%, it rose again in one moment when he decided to become Batman. All the way back up. Not in bits and pieces – all the way, all at once. Scary, isn't it? Granted, this is a fictional character, but the theory holds true, and it *is* possible for the ego to rise this quickly.

You may be wondering about something else: why did the ego of our hero actually go up when he decided to become Batman? If you recall, a person with a high ego tends to see conflict as arising from circumstances outside of him, and he focuses on engaging in this outer conflict, as opposed to engaging in self-transformation. Batman, like all superheroes, fits this description: He is focused almost exclusively on engaging in outer conflict, and usually it is conflict that is not really his own – he is actually interfering in the conflicts of others. The repercussions of his interference are starkly apparent: since outer conflicts are there to help us passively lower our egos, anyone who "solves" our challenges for us actually blocks us from receiving the gift of that ego lowering experience. As a result, the status quo is maintained, and we do not experience the transformation that the negative experience would have brought to us. In truth, to interfere in the experiences of others in the manner that a superhero does is the mark of a very high ego, because the superhero is actively enjoying the accolades and recognition he/she receives for so doing, and simultaneously perpetuating a dependence upon him/her. Batman was the Idol of Gotham – he certainly was not a humble figure. To him, surrender meant to lose, which is the way the ego always interprets it.

Let us be clear: this is not to say that it is wrong to help others. There is a big difference between helping others in a humble manner, and helping others for the sake of recognition and glory while avoiding attending to one's own inner work. If you are uncertain whether your impulse to help others comes from a place of ego or a place of love, try this simple test: would it matter to you if you never received recognition for your efforts? How does it feel to know that no one will ever thank you, or even know you did anything at all? If this would bother you, then your actions (or potential actions) are coming from a place of ego. Love does not crave recognition.

Here is another good test: in your effort to help other people, are you acting *against* some outside force, such as another group, another person, or even something as vague and amorphous as the "establishment"? Do your actions have an agenda? Or are you acting out of universal, impersonal love, with no agenda whatsoever and no concern for the ultimate outcome? This last is the only way love acts. Love never has expectations or agendas, and it never works "for" one person by working "against" another.

To illustrate this principle, at the end of *The Dark Knight*, when Bruce Wayne makes the choice to sacrifice his glory and status, his ego drops dramatically - an enormous 41 points down to 44% into the Low Ego Zone. Note that earlier on, when the woman he loved was brutally murdered after he failed to save her, his ego only dropped 12 points down to 85%, still in the High Ego Zone. Yet it takes a fantastic plunge when, in order to preserve Gotham's recently restored sense of trust in justice, he takes the rap for another man and thereby sacrifices his ego-glorifying status as super-human protector of the city and fades into hiding, a wanted man, a rejected idol, a fallen hero.

So good news! We can drop just as fast as we can rise, also through a single act. Again, doing good things for others is not bad, but if you want to keep your ego low while you do good deeds, you must refuse to glory in the attention and accolades, and you must not have a personal agenda.

Bruce Wayne's primary personal theme of ego rising is thirst for power, and his secondary theme is anger. When he was "Batman" the Idol of Gotham, he exercised a lot of power, and he vented his anger on his opponents. When he gave up his hero status and became an outlaw, not only did he give up his power as Batman; he actually became a hunted man. In this one act of self-sacrifice he overcame his most negative tendency and brought himself back to the Low Ego Zone.

For most of us the ego falls, then it rises. It falls again, only to rise again. It keeps hovering in the high ego zone, between 99% and 75%. This illustrates an important fact: it is much, much harder to retain the gains we make when we drop our ego in the High Ego Zone than in any other ego zone. The High Ego Zone is the catch-22 of ego dropping. The problem at this level is that the ego has such a grip on the psyche of the individual, he has very little ability to oppose its influence, so even when he drops it, his tendency is to allow it to go right back up. Yet this is right where he most needs to lower it, as it is where he experiences the most suffering. This brings us to the difference between *passive* ego lowering, and *active* ego lowering.

EIGHT

_____

The Medium Ego Zone and The Two Paths

The grand majority of ego lowering is performed in the passive manner. This means that a negative experience comes to the individual (see the list on page 28) and as a result, the individual's ego drops. This is what we refer to as the "Path of Pain and Suffering."

The other method of ego lowering, which we call *active* ego lowering, is much less painful. Active ego lowering means that the individual actively engages in inner transformation to lower his/her ego without the necessity of negative experiences being imposed upon him. This is the "Path of Conscious Self-Transformation."

When we reach the medium ego zone (below 75%) we are continually offered the choice to engage in inner transformation, and if the choice is not taken, only then are outer circumstances imposed. You can see here the beginning of the shift from passive to active ego lowering. Therefore, the Medium Ego Zone list is divided between these two paths: active and passive. The complete list for the Medium Ego Zone is on the next page, and note that the active path actions are in **bold**.

There is an interesting order to the events on this list, as we are first encouraged to take action on our own by a series of possible events: suffering, loss, failure. Then, we are given the opportunity to continue the journey of ego lowering on our own, without outside circumstances being imposed upon us by practicing forgiveness, non-defensiveness, non-judgment, selfless service, gratitude, surrender, equanimity, patience, renunciation, taking full responsibility, restriction, compassion, admission of wrongdoings, making amends and humility.

If we do not take the opportunities to actively drop our ego on our own, no problem. Life will take it out of our hands again – after all, Life will never let us betray ourselves! The next things that could happen are again impositions of outer

Medium Ego Zone Challenges (74%-45%)

1.	Suffering	**PASSIVE**	
2.	Loss		
3.	Failure		
4.	*Forgiveness*		A
5.	*Non-Defensiveness*		
6.	*Non-Judgment & Acceptance*		C
7.	*Selfless Service*		
8.	*Gratitude*		T
9.	*Surrender*		
10.	*Equanimity*		I
11.	*Patience*		
12.	*Renunciation*		V
13.	*Taking full responsibility*		
14.	*Restriction*		E
15.	*Compassion*		
16.	*Admission of Wrongdoing & Making Amends*		
17.	*Humility*		
18.	Humiliation		
19.	Dependency	**PASSIVE**	
20.	Incapacitation		
21.	Untimely Death		

circumstances: humiliation, dependency, incapacitation, and untimely death. Did you notice the
direct order from humility, which is an optional,
self-propelled action, and humiliation, which is an
imposed experience, immediately following it? The
message is clear: either be humble, or you will be
humiliated.

Sounds a bit threatening, but like anything in life,
it's all in how you view it. Remember, when you
have a low ego, life is much, much easier. It's
easier to be in a place of peace, to feel compassion
for all sentient beings, to accomplish good works,
to discern between healthy and unhealthy
relationships, situations and environments. It's
simply a happier place to live. So even though
these experiences are extremely difficult, they are
there to help us get over ourselves so we can get to
the good part of life.

If we look at this with the understanding that we
can actively drop our own egos, rather than
waiting for Life to do it for us, it becomes a simple
game. Such a perspective is difficult for a person
with a high ego to accept, but we have watched
people whose egos were in the high ego zone take
that positive attitude, embark on their journeys of

active self-transformation with gusto, and achieve amazing results. Anyone who begins life with an ego of 99% or lower can do it, and with a positive attitude it is much easier to do than one would ever dream possible.

NINE

The Toll For Taking the Path of Pain and Suffering: Emotional Trauma

We now come to an important issue. Dropping the ego in a passive way is damaging to the psyche, particularly to what we call the "emotional body." Is that a surprise? Probably not. When we look at the list of ways the ego can drop passively – sexual violation, legal trials, accidents, dismemberment, exile, imprisonment, etc. – it is obvious. Even the more moderate events, like emotional suffering, are traumatic to the individual. Thus we often find that the individuals who have survived the ego-lowering process in the passive manner are highly traumatized. Dropping their egos below 45% only slightly alleviates their suffering. In this case, although they no longer require Life to give them difficult external circumstances to lower their egos, they have now internalized the pain they felt from the process of dropping their egos and they continue to live in a traumatized state.

If nothing else has convinced you not to wait for the Path of Pain and Suffering, this should.

There are processes and methods we use in our practice to help traumatized individuals erase the imprint of trauma on their psyches and nervous systems, and it is completely possible to do so. We work this way with many of our clients. It's beautiful when we see formerly traumatized individuals come back to life, when we see happiness and peace return to their existence and hear the reports of life "flowing" for them again. But this scenario of lowering the ego through terrible trial, and then re-building the emotional body, is far from ideal, and we do not recommend it.

Try to imagine it this way: Life is like the Parker Brothers game of Monopoly™. Some of the ego-lowering events (with some notable exceptions) are consequences in that game – bankruptcy (financial ruin) for instance, or going straight to jail (imprisonment). If a player in the game of Monopoly were to take it seriously, it could be devastating. Even if the player was the eventual winner of the game, the road to success is usually beset by traumas of all kinds. Often, players win the game after being on the verge of bankruptcy multiple times. By the time they win, what they really want is for the game to just be over, finally.

That's like taking the Path of Pain and Suffering to passively lower your ego. By the time you drop below 45%, the time when you should really start living that life of Grace, you are so traumatized from your experiences that you may just want the game to be over already. Certainly you will be left wondering why you still can't sleep because of anxious thoughts, or why you are in a lousy relationship, or why your child is still so difficult, or why you are so depressed when you wake up in the morning.

Perhaps you married a 100% ego person because you needed your ego lowered, and he/she was just the person to do it. Not that you planned it that way. You had no idea when you married that person what you were getting out of the deal was a big dose of humbling pain, but after some time, you came to terms with that. We've actually seen cases like this. One woman married a wealthy

100% ego man and over the next 25 years her ego dropped from 97% to 25%. Interestingly, she almost left him at one point, and upon investigation, it was at the time when her ego dropped below 45%, which is the major transition to the Low Ego Zone. But she didn't leave him, because by that time she was so emotionally frozen, she was no longer aware of her own pain. Instead, she stayed, and her ego continued to drop – and her emotional body continued to shut down further. By the time her ego was at 25%, her emotional body was operating at 15%. Because she was so traumatized emotionally, she began to develop physical symptoms such as exhaustion, tremors, panic attacks and sleeplessness. It was the physical symptoms that drove her to our center for help, but it was the trauma from the passive ego lowering process that was the root cause.

As previously mentioned, all trauma imprints, no matter how bad, can be cleared. It's not easy, and it's not a pleasant process, but it is very possible. Again, however, this is not the ideal route, and it is certainly not the one we recommend. This woman did a lot of work to recover her emotional body, and because of the place she was in with her marriage, it took an enormous amount of courage to recognize that as she healed her emotional self, she would most likely find herself moving away from the financial safety and security that her otherwise dreadful marriage provided her. No matter how you cut it, it wasn't the easy road – passive, in this sense, is a much, much harder road.

This is one of the key points: seek to actively lower your own ego. Choose the path of conscious self-transformation. Take another look at the bold items on the list on page 53 and make of it a daily practice. Win the Game of Life joyfully, actively and with style. It is so very possible and so beautiful to see. It is much easier and faster than you would ever have imagined.

Let's compare that case with another one. We had a client who was born with an ego at 85%. Despite a difficult and traumatic childhood, it only dropped 10 points to 75% until her fifty-fourth year, when she began to heal herself from some old emotional trauma. Healing trauma and letting go of the past is one of the ways we can recover those ego points that we lost as a result of not taking responsibility and missing 90-day deadlines. As a result of that healing, her ego dropped from 75% to

74%, out of the High Ego Zone. When people drop out of the high ego zone they begin to see life very differently, and in this case, she became aware that her romantic partnership was not the loving partnership she craved, and she broke it off. She was unprepared for what followed: a nasty, expensive, and lengthy legal battle with the now ex-partner that threatened to result in bankruptcy.

It was at this point that she came to see us, while the matter was still unresolved. When we investigated, we found that her former partner was a 97% ego, and when our client dropped out of the High Ego Zone, they were no longer compatible with one another, which was why she was compelled to break it off. However, because she had chosen to not take full responsibility for that decision but instead to feel a victim of the ex-partner, her ego had stayed stuck at 74%. You see, your ego can only fall, even in the passive mode, when you let go of your victim stance. After meeting with us and gaining a thorough understanding of the situation and what she specifically needed to do in order to pro-actively speed up the process, she went away and spent two months transforming herself. She came back to our office a changed woman, and her ego was now at 44%. The situation with the ex-partner now no longer troubled her the way it did before, and she understood that even though the situation had not changed, she had changed, and that was what was important. She was now also keenly aware of how badly she had handled the situation when she broke off the relationship (at this point she was still in the medium ego zone, and in that place we are generally still acting from a place of ego, even though it is less pronounced than in the high ego zone).

Her case illustrates one of the most important things about entering a state of Grace: anything that can happen to a person with a high ego can happen to a person with a low ego, the only difference is in the way the person with a low ego perceives and responds to the circumstance. The low ego person can be at peace regardless of the external picture (and the lower the ego goes, the more pronounced this peace becomes), whereas the high ego person cannot. This is the crucial difference.

This story has a fascinating conclusion. About three months after this woman had managed to reach the low ego zone, her ex-partner (who was also a client of ours), came to our office unexpectedly, with no appointment. Many things had happened in her life since the break-up, and as a result, her ego had dropped from 97% to 74%, out of the high ego zone. She now found that any urge she'd had to continue the struggle with her ex-partner was now gone, and all she wanted was to be peacefully rid of the situation. Although she had refused to have any contact or communication with her ex-partner in two years, she was now willing to meet and not only compromise, but make an extremely generous offer. Guess which ego lowering strategy came up as the best one for her to employ? "Admission of wrongdoing and making amends."

She walked out of our office and was waiting to check out with our receptionist when her ex walked in, also unexpectedly and without an appointment. The healing of the two-year situation began right there in our waiting room, no lawyers, arbitrators, or judges required.

This is what happens when we lower our egos.

TEN

Practical Ego Lowering Strategies for Everyone

The first question we all have when we receive this information is, "so how can I lower my ego the fastest, most painless way possible? Is that an option or am I doomed to have some unpleasant experiences?"

The exciting, joyful answer to this question is YES! It is possible to lower your ego quickly, efficiently, and relatively painlessly. Although we are each ultimately destined to have low egos, none of us is destined to suffer. Suffering is completely optional.

So how do you do it? Well, take a look at the list on the next page. It shows how many points we drop for each of the passive ego-lowering experiences.

This list is a bit disappointing. It makes it seem like it is so hard to drop one's ego! It's difficult to

Passive Ego Lowering Experiences: Points Dropped

1.	Suffering	1-20 pts
2.	Loss	1-15 pts
3.	Failure	1-15 pts
4.	Submission	1-15 pts
5.	Humiliation	1-15 pts
6.	Violence	1-15 pts
7.	Incapacitation	1-15 pts
8.	Dependency	1-10 pts
9.	Involuntary Caretaking	1-5 pts
10.	Domination (for females) / Emasculation (for males)	1-15 pts
11.	Divorce	1-10 pts
12.	Exile / Banishment	1-5 pts
13.	Financial Ruin	1-10 pts
14.	Accidents	1-15 pts

Passive Ego Lowering -cont.
Experiences: Points Dropped

15. Legal Trials   1-10 pts

16. Imprisonment   5-20 pts

     a. Life in prison, innocent of the crime: 20 pts

     b. Life in prison, guilty of the crime: 15 pts

     c. Under 2 years in prison, guilty or innocent: 5 pts

     d. Over 2 years, but less than life, guilty or innocent: 10 pts

17. Sexual Violation   5-15 pts

18. Dismemberment   15 pts

19. Untimely Death   10-15 pts

     a. For the person who dies: 10 pts

     b. For the people who are left behind when someone else dies an untimely death: 15 pts

20. Torture   5-15 pts

21. Murder / Execution
(guilty or innocent, it's the same)   20 pts

believe that if you go to jail for less than two years, it doesn't matter if you are guilty or innocent – you lose the same number of ego points either way, but that is how it is. It's not really necessary to analyze in detail, for this much is clear: taking the passive road to ego lowering is a very long, very painful journey.

Now let's take a look at how many points we drop when we engage our will and actively destroy our own egos. It turns out that this is much simpler, for we reduce our egos **one point for each and every incident, episode or moment** of any of the actions on the list on the next page.

So let's recap: while serving life in prison for a crime we didn't commit will only drop our ego twenty points, we can drop *one* point for every moment where we consciously let go of hatred, self-righteousness, impatience, reactivity, ingratitude, etc. and call on our higher selves to help us forgive, to be non-defensive, to resist judgment of others, or to exercise patience (or any of the other actions on the list on the next page). *One point!*

Active Ego Lowering Practices

1. Forgiveness

2. Non-Defensiveness

3. Non-Judgment & Acceptance

4. Selfless Service

5. Gratitude

6. Surrender

7. Equanimity

8. Patience

9. Renunciation

10. Taking full responsibility

11. Restriction

12. Compassion

13. Admission of Wrongdoing & Making Amends

14. Humility

What this means is that one could drop twenty points in a single day. However, our ego also rises, as mentioned previously. Ego rising works just the same way: we go up one point for every moment that we give in to one of the ego-rising impulses (lack of discipline, lack of love, ingratitude, feeling superior, wanting power or dominance, anger or resentment, substance abuse or addiction). So what most of our egos do is bob up and down all day long, hovering around some "set point." We have a moment of patience, where we resist honking at the car in front of us even though the light CLEARLY turned green three seconds ago; we give an extra hug to someone we wouldn't normally hug or we bite our tongues instead of lashing back when someone accuses us. These things all drop us a point. The problem is that most of us then gain that point right back because we figure we've done our good deed for the day and we go right back to our old patterns of behavior. So on we go, sustaining precisely the same ego level with which we began the day.

It is for this reason that most of us eventually call to ourselves a passive ego lowering experience, because we need the experience to drop us to a new "set point." For instance, someone might have an ego around 97% although it bounces up and down throughout the day, dropping a point here, gaining it back there. For this person, achieving permanent ego drops through self-discipline might just seem impossible, so instead she (unconsciously) waits until a car accident, divorce, a death, or some other major event takes place that gives her a big drop all at once. Then she hovers around that new set point (if she doesn't hold on to self-righteous anger or a victim mentality, which will send her right back to where she was) until something else comes to drop her further. Remember Guy.

Again, the trick is to exercise discipline, or spiritual will, and here is the key: you just have to do one more instance of forgiveness, or gratitude, or non-defensiveness, or any of the other things on the list, every day, just one more. It's a change of one degree, but as we journey through our lives like ships on the sea, one degree will land us hundreds of miles from where we would have gone.

Let this point not be lost: we are not talking about perfection. We are talking about just a bit more mindfulness, a little extra effort. That's all the discipline that is required. We don't have to be perfect. We just have to improve incrementally, and the changes will be dramatic and swift.

ELEVEN

The Low Ego Zone

What about people who go below 45%? Remember, it is possible to go all the way to 0%. Think of what it would be like to live without seeing life through the veil of the ego! Imagine the peace, the feeling of connection to all other life. Really - try to imagine what that would be like. So, why don't more people work to achieve that?

The list of ways to drop the ego below 45% is short, and deceptively simple. See the list on the next page.

Let's pause and consider this list for a moment. This list is for those people who, by our society's standards, already have very, very low egos. In fact, only 5% of the population has an ego below 45%, and most of that 5% is just barely into the Low Ego Zone. Do you think this list is easy to accomplish for them? No, it is not. This path is a

Ego Clearing

1.   Equanimity (non-reactivity)

2.   Restriction

3.   Forgiveness

4.   Patience

5.   Taking Full Responsibility

6.   Humility

7.   Surrender

journey to an almost completely ego-less existence, where we do not react to anything in our life, where we are willing to restrict escapist, self-sabotaging, self-destructive behavior, where we take full responsibility for everything, absolutely everything in our life, and where we practice forgiveness, patience, humility, and surrender in trust to the flow of Life.

If you think about it, what we have just described is the picture that we all wish our parents had conformed to. It's what we expect from the President and our other world leaders. It's what we want from our bosses, coaches and other superiors. We now realize just how ridiculous these expectations are, in light of another important fact: 60% of the world's population has an ego above 75%. In other words, more than half of the people we are likely to encounter have egos in the high ego zone and most of the rest are struggling in the middle ego zone. The reason people who actually do drop their egos to below 45%– and keep them there - stand out to us is because such individuals are so rare. The good news is that such low-ego people are becoming more common. Not *commonplace*, but there are more and more of them every year, and we are moving into an age when they will become commonplace. Can you imagine what the world will look like then?

By observing our clients as they drop into the low ego zone we have made an important discovery: everyone knows when it happens to them. All of our low-ego clients report that they felt the shift when their ego score dropped below 45% and furthermore, that almost immediately their external circumstances changed in some way. Perhaps a troubled relationship suddenly got smoother, or a dream job opened up for them, their health improved, or they suddenly noticed a lessening in their financial pressures. Were these changes simply changes in perception on the part of the client, or were they objective changes in the world outside the client? Our answer is both, for our outer world is inextricably bound to our inner perception.

TWELVE

Going The Extra Mile: Dropping Into the Very Low Ego Zone

Up to now, we have discussed ego dropping in the sense that it is a necessary step to take in order to live a more peaceful, graceful life. Yet there is more to it than that: at a certain point, dropping one's ego below 45% creates a major spiritual shift.

When we drop below 45%, into the Low Ego Zone, we begin to live life under Grace, and this is a significant change from before, because we begin to find that we are free of most of the major issues that used to threaten to derail our lives (see the High Ego and Medium Ego zone lists), and when difficult circumstances do arise, we view them in a different light. But there is another, further step to take, and that is from living under Grace to living life in complete surrender to our divine purpose.

Although lowering the ego at any time is a challenge, this is the hardest drop, because this is the point where we must surrender all sense of having a separate ego, identity, or personality. This is where we must surrender even our occasional worry or our periodic episodes with latent ego. Up to this point, we are moving in a gradual way towards a life that is more and more surrendered to our divine purpose, but at the point where we shift into the lowest state of ego, we make a clear jump into living in a constant state of surrender.

There is a pattern to lowering the ego: the higher the ego, the harder it is to get the courage and determination to lower it, but the easier it is to lower. Yet the lower the ego, the greater the benefit for each point lowered. A shift from 24% to 23%, for instance, is extremely significant for the person making the shift, much more significant than a drop from 98% to 97%.

This is an important thing to remember, because simply following most moral systems and many religious theologies will only lead us to the gates of the Low Ego Zone, (45% ego) which is to say, by following those rules we become good human beings. Now, that is a wonderful thing to be and a decent way to live, but it is not the end of the journey, for the best is still to come. This is where we depart from simple religious or moral life and go deep within into our own individual spirituality. The closer one draws to 0% ego, the more one feels a deep and abiding sense of peace that goes beyond words. A person with an ego at 44% simply lives a life free from most major conflicts. A person with an ego at 5% lives a life nestled in the heart of God, and anyone who comes near such a person is aware of it.

Once a person has dropped her ego to the low ego zone, the challenge to lower it further changes in nature. This person is coming closer and closer to a true, constant, clear connection with her Source of life, and in order to go even closer, she must begin to consciously release all last vestiges of her belief that she is here on earth to *do anything*. She is not here to do anything; she is here to be a channel for pure consciousness. There is nothing else for her to do, and any attempt on her part to "do" anything will take her farther from her Source. Once we achieve this level, we begin to understand that the true purpose of our lives is to be expressions of pure consciousness. This is an endless blessing not only to ourselves but also to all with whom we come into contact. This is the final stage of complete surrender, and while it sounds frightening to us when we have higher egos, the closer we come to this stage, the more we understand the pull to go further and further into ego-less existence. The source of all our troubles is our need to make something of our small selves. The answer to all of our deepest longings lies in conscious union with our Source, which can only be achieved when our ego is no longer present (or nearly not) and cannot interfere.

THIRTEEN

How Trauma Keeps Us Locked in the Past

It is not possible to reach a very low level of ego if you are still holding on to trauma. The reason is simple: trauma keeps us locked in the past, which is to say, in linear time. Only the ego exists in linear time. Grace exists in the eternal, omnipresent *now*. Just as we can either be ruled by the ego or in a state of Grace, but not both, we can either be present now or living in the past/future – but not both simultaneously.

How does trauma keep us locked in the past? When we are traumatized, it affects us not only emotionally but physiologically as well. We literally store the trauma in both our bodies and psyches – in our nervous system as well as in our muscles and tissues. What this trauma imprint does is keep us enslaved to the reaction we had to whatever event caused it. Until we remove the trauma not only from our psyches but from our physiology we will continue to hold on to the pattern we adopted as a response to the trauma, long after the situation itself has been resolved.

This "trauma imprint" keeps us reacting to new situations as though they were repeats of the old situations that originally traumatized us. When people come to us for help with an emotional issue we often find the reason they have been unable to resolve it is that they stopped growing emotionally at a very young age – their emotional body stayed at that age. One of the common ages for people to become stuck is twelve or thirteen, which is typically the onset of puberty. Invariably, people who are stuck there experienced a major trauma at that age and have never been able to release it, even though they may not be consciously aware of it. This prevents them from making a complete transition from childhood to emotional maturity.

Often, the traumas people experience that keep their emotional bodies stuck in the past are not things they think of as severe. In fact, most of our clients tell us they believe they are already "over that," until we measure the charge they still have from the trauma and they see that it remains very high – often 99 or 100 percent, which means they haven't dropped any of the charge at all since it happened. Although they may have made mental sense of what occurred, the trauma from it is still lodged in their nervous system and it gets re-awakened every time something happens in the present that echoes that experience, or triggers a similar response on their part.

The traumas we have uncovered in our clients that have kept them emotionally stuck in adolescence range from seemingly minor ones such as a parental divorce or moving schools and not being accepted by the "in" crowd, to more severe ones such as being exposed to abandonment, abuse and death. Interestingly, even the ones that appear to be more minor in nature arouse a similar residual dysfunction in the nervous system. One gentleman recalled that his father had pocketed all the money he received as gifts for his bar mitzvah. To an adult mind these may not seem like such powerful events, but to a young adolescent they can be extremely traumatic and often result in a life-long loss of trust in life and other people.

What we see with people who are stuck emotionally in the past is very interesting. The first thing is that they tend to respond to stressful situations by reverting to their emotional age. For example, if a woman is stuck emotionally at twelve, then when she has a conflict with someone, she reverts to the age of twelve in the way that she responds to and deals with the conflict. Perhaps you have noticed this transformation in yourself or in your partner when you found yourselves in an argument and realized that you were both behaving like children? It is not an uncommon occurrence -most of us have unresolved trauma, and very few people have an emotional age that matches their chronological age.

Yet what happens when we resolve the original trauma that kept us locked at that young age is even more interesting: we will be more present with what is really happening in the *now*, and not only will we be able to respond in a more mature way, our ego will drop points. Holding onto trauma is a function of the ego. When the trauma is released, so is the ego that held on to it (there are many trauma release techniques available to assist in releasing trauma, see Appendix C for more information).

So trauma, ego, and linear time are all interlinked, and they all prevent us from living in the present moment. There is no way to achieve a true, ultimate state of Grace if you are not in the present moment, because Grace exists now. Grace does not exist in the past, nor does it exist in the future. In fact, nothing exists in the past or in the future. The only time is now. A person with a very low ego lives life in a state of Grace, which means she lives almost completely in the present moment, without thoughts about the past or worries or concern for the future. So trauma is more than painful: it prevents us from achieving a state of Grace.

FOURTEEN

Latent Ego

It is possible to have an ego in the low ego zone and still have reactions to life that register as very high on the ego scale. This is where life gets tricky, and this is one of the reasons we emphasize that it is important not only to have a low ego, but also to be emotionally healthy and to let go of past traumas.

When our ego is in the low ego zone, we are generally moral people. We are civic-minded, law-abiding, decent citizens. But despite this general "goodness," there can be hidden sides to our personalities that come out when old traumas are triggered.

When something happens that we don't like, we always have options as to how we respond to the event, and it is our response that determines whether we carry trauma from the event forward into our lives – or not. Most importantly, it is the level of our resistance to the event that will decide whether the event becomes traumatic, or if it fades into memory as just another thing that happened.

Let's take an example situation to illustrate how this works. This example deals with a woman who made the choice to carry childhood trauma forward into her adult life. This woman's ego is in the low ego zone and she loves to buy shoes. While growing up, she was never able to afford to buy them, and this lowered her ego considerably. Now, she is married and successful, and she can afford to buy all the shoes she wants. Her natural instinct is to buy shoes every week; her husband feels this is excessive. Yet every time he casually mentions that she might be overdoing it on the shoes, she gets triggered. She gets angry with him and throws the full force of her anger out, accusing him of trying to deprive her, of being cheap, of being unkind and cruel. After all, it's only shoes, isn't it? Why shouldn't she have as many as she wants, since she didn't get them when she was growing up?

Well, there are a lot of reasons she shouldn't have as many as she wants, and the first one is because it isn't helping her – it is feeding her belief in her own trauma. We don't let go of trauma by overcompensating for it; we let go of trauma by *letting it go*. What is interesting about this is that we have tested people while they were in the midst of a triggered state and their egos registered at up to 97%, even if normally the ego score was in the low ego zone. This is a clear sign of a trauma that has stayed with us and is still (unconsciously) governing our lives and directing our behavior and emotions in some way.

When this woman was deprived of buying shoes as a young woman, it lowered her ego because it forced her to restrict her self-indulgence. But her response to this ego-lowering experience was to feel deprived, instead of being grateful that her ego was being lowered. Rather than searching for a deeper form of contentment to help her get over her disappointment in her lack of shoes, she decided to feel pain, and she hid that pain away in a special place in her psyche and nursed it. Her ego told her she was justified in feeling deprived and that one day she would have the chance to "express herself" and then she would make up for all that time she suffered. We call this *latent ego*. Latent ego is tied in to unresolved trauma, and even after one is in the low ego zone, it can come back to haunt you.

Going back to the Shoe Woman: it is obvious that buying more shoes isn't what she wants; what she really wants is to stop feeling the pain of that latent trauma. Buying more shoes only offers temporary relief– that's why she keeps buying more. What would make her feel better would be to let go of the trauma she is still holding, and she may need some help to do that. She isn't truly conscious of what is happening, which is why she lashes out at her husband and projects her feeling of deprivation onto him. Once she lets go of the trauma, however, her unending need to buy shoes will disappear, and the shoes that she does get will give her much more pleasure, because she will be buying them because she likes them, not because she thinks (unconsciously) they will resolve her trauma for her.

There is another way to approach this problem, which is through the lens of the ego. Trauma and ego are simply two lenses through which we view the same core problem; it's just that sometimes it's easier to conceptualize the problem as ego, and sometimes it is easier to conceptualize the problem as trauma. In this case, either view would work. Although this woman's ego is in the low ego zone, in this particular circumstance, her ego shoots up to the high ego zone due to the effect of latent ego, which is the result of unresolved trauma. So if we view this situation through the lens of the ego, what comes up as the solution? Restriction. Ironically, this is what caused the trauma in the first place – the fact that she was restricted from buying shoes as a child. In this case, however, the restriction was imposed; it was not by choice. It was the result of being on the Path of Pain and Suffering, rather than the Path of Conscious Self-Transformation. The resistance the woman held to the imposed restriction caused her to feel pain and to store this pain as trauma, which became latent ego. Again, this illustrates how lowering the ego in the passive manner tends to cause emotional issues, whereas when we take charge and lower the ego on our own, we don't suffer from trauma.

Sometimes the way to resolve trauma is simply to refuse to allow it to hijack us. To do this takes what we call discipline, or spiritual will. This is the conscious part of the process of resolving this issue: we must stand firm, and restrict the impulse that threatens to overtake us. This is an act of will and discipline. Some part of the trauma may need to be resolved on an unconscious level through some other sort of process. But it is clear that at least one thing the Shoe Woman needs to do is restrict her compulsion to purchase shoes. That is where her responsibility for her own process begins. It may be that she has a further responsibility to work with someone to release the unconscious part of the trauma as well, but it is undeniable that her first step is to practice restriction.

Many people find this difficult to do.

FIFTEEN

Taking Full Responsibility

Another way to achieve this state of low, low ego is to take full and complete responsibility for everything in your life, from your birth right through to the present moment. As we work through our past traumas and latent ego reactions, which is a necessary step to take if one wants to clear the ego completely, one fact begins to become clear to us: the very things that traumatized us were the things that we called to ourselves in order to lower our own egos, and we were traumatized not by the events themselves, but by our *reactions* to those events. In fact, the easiest way to understand this is that the level of our trauma was directly proportional to the level of our resistance.

Let's illustrate this with an analogy. Suppose you were sitting in the front passenger seat of a car when the car got into an accident. Imagine you saw the accident coming, realized you were going to hit the car in front of you and instinctively reacted by straightening your legs and bracing them against the front of the car. As a result of this resistance, when the impact occurred, both of your legs were injured.

Now, imagine responding a different way. Let's say you were very relaxed when this happened, and although you saw the accident coming, you had the presence of mind to resist the impulse to protect yourself by reactively bracing your legs out in front of you. Instead you bent your knees and raised them out of the way; you did the opposite of what your "survival" instinct told you to do by accessing your higher consciousness. In this scenario, your legs escaped without harm.

In both scenarios, your physical trauma was directly proportional to the amount of physical resistance you offered up to the situation. This analogy is apropos to any situation where Life offers you the chance to lower your ego - the more you resist the opportunity, the greater the trauma you will carry around with you as a result.

We don't say this lightly. We are only too aware of the reactions this statement will bring: What do you mean, don't resist? Do you mean I should not have resisted when I was raped? How can you say that a four year-old child is responsible for resisting the pain of her parents' divorce? Oh yes, we know this sounds outrageous. It seems to go against everything our society believes about holding perpetrators accountable for their crimes and it also appears to "blame the victim." Let us address these concerns.

First of all, we must remember that the trauma is of our own making: we created it through our own resistance, we carried it around with us for some length of time, and we are the only ones that have the power to remove it and let it go. It was never inflicted upon us as a punishment. So whether it was "our fault" or not - whether we knew better or not - we still have it, and it's up to us to remove it if we want to move forward. This is what we mean by taking total responsibility: we must recognize and consciously accept that every single one of the experiences in our lives that we previously believed we were justified in being self-righteously angry or defensive about was actually nothing more than an opportunity Life generously offered to us to lower our ego. Unless we get over our resistance to that truth, we will never move forward.

Furthermore, we aren't saying that someone who commits a crime shouldn't be brought to justice – of course they should, that's how they will eventually lower their ego. What we are saying is that each and every one of us will have to one day *accept total responsibility for our reactions to the experiences of our lives* if we want to drop our egos to the lowest level possible. Remember, responsibility is not the same as blame; so taking responsibility isn't about accepting or placing blame. This isn't a judgment against anyone; it is a simple truth we must accept. Once we accept it, however, we see just how empowering it is, because it means that we are not, never were and never will be, a victim of any other person or circumstance.

If you have a pebble in your shoe, do you refuse to take it out because you believe someone else put it there, or because you believe it isn't your fault it is there? No, you stop, take off your shoe, and shake the pebble out. Why? Why don't you have to think it through, try to figure out how the pebble got there, and whose fault it is that it is there?

The answer is simple: because it is completely obvious to you that the solution to your problem is to get rid of the pebble. You don't need to know whose fault it is the pebble is there, nor do you care. You don't even need to know if it was your own fault or not, you just need to get rid of the pebble and then you'll never think about that pebble again.

It is the same with trauma. You don't need to figure out whose fault the trauma was; in fact, doing so will only keep you from letting it go. You don't need to know if it was your fault or not, or if you knew better or not at the time – you just need to let it go so that you can stop suffering, just like taking the pebble out of your shoe allows you to walk forward without pain.

It is possible to be raped and forgive your rapist. It is possible to have horrible crimes perpetrated against you, your family, or your people and to forgive your tormentors. It is not only possible; it is the way to become free of the experience. It is necessary for your continuing development and your continuing progression towards a life of Truth to do so, and furthermore, to be grateful for what the experience brought you, which is the same in all such cases: it lowered your ego, and thereby brought you closer to a state of Grace.

Most of us pick up a lot of pebbles in our shoes on our way to Grace. Let's not sit around like petulant children, arguing over who put which pebbles in whose shoes, or how long they've been there, or holding on to them as keepsakes. Let's just shake out our shoes and move on, for the best part of life is right in front of us and there's no need to waste any more time.

SIXTEEN

There Is an Alternative to Trauma

Is there a way to lower the ego passively without serious emotional trauma? Can we lower our ego without getting a lot of pebbles in our shoes? It would seem so. There are a couple of requirements though, and the first is that we be emotionally healthy, which means that we love and accept ourselves fully. An individual with a strong emotional body may not necessarily know how to lower her ego on her own, but when Life gives her opportunity to lower it, she takes the opportunity, takes charge, and refuses to feel like a victim.

Let's look at an example of someone who lowered her ego passively and without serious emotional trauma. Sometimes we find our greatest examples in what might seem like the simplest characters. But, as we shall see, being simple isn't the same as being stupid, even though many people confuse the two (thus the innumerable blond jokes that are often exchanged in our society). So, let's just take a look at one of those "dumb" blonds, shall we? We now turn our attention to the character Elle Woods from the movie *Legally Blonde*[4].

(Authors' Note: we are aware that Elle is a fictional character, and that certain events in this movie are totally implausible. However, once again her character represents a true archetype, and the silliness just makes it more entertaining, it doesn't detract from the reality of the archetypal lesson).

If you are familiar with the story, you remember that many different things happened over the course of this movie to help beat Elle's ego down. Although she was the star of the show as an undergraduate (beautiful, great student, president of her sorority), she was an outcast at Harvard Law School. She had difficulty keeping up with her classes; she was made the butt of jokes and excluded by her classmates. Werner, her "true

---

[4] Luketic, R., (Director), Kidney, R. (Producer), & Brown, A., Lutz, K, Smith, K. (Writers). (2007), *Legally Blonde* [DVD], United States: 20th Century Fox Home Entertainment. (Original Release date 2001).

love" and the man for whom she had worked so hard to get into Harvard Law School, proposed to another woman. It would seem that none of her plans worked out.

Perhaps the best scene in the movie is when she attends a party that a snide girl told her was to be a costume party, only to find that she is the only one in costume, and a Playboy Bunny costume at that. Elle doesn't run away in tears, nor does she show the slightest sign of embarrassment. Nor, it must be noted, does she denounce her nemesis (Werner's fiancé, the girl who set her up to believe it was a costume party) in public. Instead, she casually takes a drink and laughs the whole situation off as a joke. Such a performance takes remarkable emotional confidence, and that is the real key here. Throughout the movie, Elle's emotional body remains at a very high 90%. It is because of her emotional health that she is able to roll with the punches and make changes in herself when she sees that she needs to, rather than blaming others or getting caught up in anger or self-hatred.

When Life hands a challenge to Elle, she doesn't vent her anger outward, or engage in battle with people or situations outside of herself. Neither does she turn her anger toward herself and get caught up in depression. Instead, she takes action and responds by making inner changes. For instance, when Werner tells her she isn't smart enough for him, she decides to study hard and get into Harvard Law School. When she accomplishes that and finds he still isn't impressed, she makes a shift inside herself again and begins to take her law studies seriously. Imagine what her other options were: she could have decided that Werner was a loser, that she hated him and that he had hurt her irreparably, gone on to hold onto that emotional trauma without making any changes in herself and gone on anti-depressant medication. She could have decided that Werner's snotty little fiancé was the real problem and devoted herself to sabotaging the other woman. The list of alternative options involving ego-rising behavior is endless, and all of them involve self-sabotage. But Elle always chose the path of inner transformation, and she triumphed in the end, successfully lowering her ego while remaining emotionally healthy.

This is one of the most common themes in movies and other types of storytelling - the age-old story of redemption. As the foregoing example illustrates, this typically happens for the protagonist through some sort of self-transformation brought on by difficult (ego-destroying) experiences. As a result of this ego lowering process the character reaches emotional maturity and perhaps becomes more open to love and compassion.

The reason why it can be so useful to look at fictional characters that resonate with audiences is because we can see the inner stories of their lives in a way that we simply cannot observe real people unless they are close personal friends. Even then, most of us don't have the kind of observational skills it takes to pick out the significant events that shape a life from the endless minutia. This is where a talented storyteller is invaluable, for they show us enough to help us relate to an archetype with which we are already subconsciously familiar without boring us with unimportant details.

Try this yourself: watch your favorite movie and see if you can identify the ego zones of the main characters. Notice if what befalls the characters conforms to what you would expect based on those different zones. Also observe if you are more drawn to movies and books where the characters drop their egos through active means. Most of us have a deep and intrinsic appreciation for such stories.

So we have now discussed a number of things: The Ego, the Ego Power scale, the five levels of the Ego Power Scale, how the ego rises, the difference between the Path of Pain and Suffering (passive ego lowering) and the Path of Conscious Self Transformation (active ego lowering), and how holding on to trauma keeps us enslaved to our latent ego.

That's a lot of information about the ego, but it turns out that it's just the beginning. What we didn't know when we began our research is that there is such a thing as a group ego, and it behaves similarly to individual egos, except on a larger scale. Since we are all participants in at least one and generally many more than one group ego, it behooves us to understand this as well. We now move on to discuss group egos, how group egos interact with each other, and how we as individuals interact with the larger group egos of which we are a part.

II. GROUP EGO

SEVENTEEN

Understanding Group Behavior

When I was an undergraduate student at UC Berkeley in the mid 1990's, I was often the only blond person in my classes. Fellow students regularly asked if I was at Berkeley as part of an Affirmative Action program for blonds ("Ah yes!" you may be thinking. "That's why she chose Elle Woods as an example..." Yes it is. I could relate to her). My chosen field of study was the Middle East, specifically Palestinian-Israeli relations, and the question I was most often posed by everyone I met was, "Why on earth are you studying that?" quickly followed by, "Are you Jewish?"

I am not Jewish. It would probably come as less of a shock today to see a white, middle-class girl from Southern California studying Arabic given the events that began with 911 and continue on with the war in Iraq. But in the mid-1990s, the classes I took on the Middle East at Berkeley were populated almost entirely with students of Middle Eastern origin who had a personal relationship to the material. What everyone wanted to know was, if I wasn't Jewish, then what was my connection to the Middle East?

My answer was difficult for most people to digest. "I want to understand the nature of group conflict," I would reply, and watch as the questioner's expression changed from curiosity to either amusement or boredom. Group conflict was not a hot topic in an era where undergrads from Berkeley that studied computer science could have a starting salary of $75,000 to $100,000 at their pick of Silicon Valley companies. Group conflict was one of those topics that led, if one was lucky, to further, unpaid research in grad school, or if one was less lucky, to an unpaid internship shuffling paperwork in an NGO somewhere.

Nevertheless, I pursued my study of group conflict diligently. I traveled to Israel and Palestine and spent time visiting places that no tourist ever sees- a Palestinian Human Rights organization in Ramallah, for instance, or a church project for women in the Gaza Strip. I stayed overnight with families. I visited Israeli settlers in fortified enclaves. I toured a UN Refugee camp and interviewed Bedouins of a beleaguered tribe whose land had been expropriated. I met with Israeli and Palestinian scholars, authors, and magazine editors. Ultimately, I left more confused than I was when I arrived, for I was now very sure of two things: everyone I had met with wanted an end to the conflict, and yet it was unlikely that this would have any influence over the situation whatsoever. In short, it didn't matter that people on both sides wished for peace: conflict persisted.

Back at Berkeley, I participated in a dialogue group with Palestinian, Israeli, Jewish, Arab, and Muslim students. I was asked to give a slide show and talk about my experiences at a few different forums. In cooperation with the other students in the dialogue group (representing all sides of the conflict), I organized a public forum to help educate others about the issues and pave the way for civilized discussion of a political topic so hot that students on campus often felt threatened by the actions of their politically-charged peers. The forum, although a success in the eyes of the organizers, was attacked in a newspaper as being "Anti-Semitic," despite the heavy involvement of several Jewish organizers. The dialogue group, which had seemed to make so much progress between the participating members, disbanded in disappointment. Again, individual change was made, but when those individuals sought to expand that change to a group level, we were stopped in our tracks.

By my senior year, I was as confused as ever about the nature of group conflict and why it persists since all of my experience taught me that if the group level would only reflect the individual level, conflict would end. Individuals may wish for peace and can overcome prejudices to see the humanity in the opposition. Yet even when this happens on the individual level, as I saw in Israel and Palestine, it is not necessarily reflected on the group level. After all my studies, I still could not understand why group conflict would persist in the face of individual willingness to compromise, other than a vague feeling that there were powerful, entrenched interests that stood to gain a great deal from perpetuating conflict. Yet even that theory was a difficult one to prove, and indeed I was never convinced of it – it was more like a conspiracy theory that neatly explained everything without really explaining anything.

I wrote an honors thesis but was so disheartened by my own failure to answer the original question I had posed at the beginning of my studies that I removed it from the school library without permission and never returned it. My disappointment in myself and in this fundamental failure led to a complete abandonment of the entire topic. I stopped watching the news on the Middle East and started reading about other, more understandable, topics, and went on to get a Master's in Organizational Management and Psychology, working with small groups in business to help them resolve individual differences in working styles and communication. It seemed to me that such resolution strategies only worked on the micro level, not on the macro level. But the question of how to resolve group conflict never entirely left my mind, and the discovery of *group ego* was what finally led to a deeper understanding of this issue.

Remarkably, countries have egos, religions have egos, all institutions and organizations have egos. A Little League team has an ego. Any grouping or gathering of people has its own "group ego." This group ego is not the average of all the individual egos that make up the group. It is its own entity, and engagement with a group, or between groups, means engagement with the egos of those groups.

It is important to remember that the ego of a group does not necessarily reflect the egos of the individuals that make up the group. There may be a loose relationship, because a group made up of individuals whose egos were all under 45% would likely have a low group ego, and likewise a group made up of 100% individual egos is guaranteed to have a 100% ego, but these are extreme examples and we don't know of any such groups that exist in the real world. Most groups are made up of a mixture of individuals, and so it is possible that an individual with an ego under 45% could belong to a group that has an ego of 100%. For instance, there were low-ego Germans in Nazi Germany. Although they belonged to a group with an ego of 100%, as individuals, their egos were lower. Therefore, it is important to never generalize from a group ego down to the individual level. Do not assume that all Germans in Nazi Germany were 100%. Clearly, many were not, and some even risked their lives to help the persecuted.

Also, it is important to recognize that we are part of any group ego with which we associate our identity. If we are American, then we are part of the American group ego. This is much less a conscious choice than one would think. We cannot dissociate ourselves from the American group ego simply by saying we don't want to be a part of it – it takes a lot more effort than that. In order to understand how to remove oneself from a group ego (which is a desirable thing to do) let's try to understand how group egos work.

Group egos work basically the same way individual egos work: they can be lowered actively or passively (the Path of Conscious Transformation vs. the Path of Pain and Suffering) and the passive ways a group ego can be reduced are the same as those for an individual ego. One notable thing about country egos (which are a kind of group ego) is that they can only go as low as 30%. This is because in order for the group ego to go lower, the institution of a "nation-state" would have to dissolve. Group egos under 30% do not need a state to govern them. As humanity makes the transition to lower and lower group egos, the nation-state system will (we believe) eventually dissolve, and a different form of order will arise.

If a group ego can be made up of individuals with wildly diverging individual egos, then how, you may ask, can you tell how high a group ego is, unless (like us) you have a tool with which to measure it? The answer is that a group ego is the measure of how that group *acts* in its dealings with other groups. In other words, it is not how the individuals in that group act, or how the individuals *want* their group to act – it is how the group actually takes action (or doesn't) in the world. A group ego is the reflection of the *actions* of the group.

Let us draw an analogy. When we as individuals are faced with a stressful situation, we often find that we have competing impulses (this is what creates the stress) that are almost like different voices in our head trying to out-shout one another. One voice will tell us to do one thing, a different voice will advise an alternate action. Often, the wisest voice inside our head will be the quietest one – it's the ego's voice that is loudest. The level of our ego is determined by the amount of time we spend listening to the voice of the ego, and acting on its behalf. Remember, that is precisely what the ego scale is – it is *a measure of how much time we are acting out the will of the ego.*

In the same way, in any group there are bound to be differences of opinion – different voices crying out for different actions. The ego of the group is ultimately determined by which voices it follows. This is why a group can have a high ego and yet include many members of very low ego – again, it is often the voices of the lowest egos that are the softest, and the voices of the highest egos that are the loudest and most insistent, and which are therefore obeyed.

The lists of ways group egos can be reduced are the same as the lists for individual egos, but of course, the way a group ego is dismembered or executed takes a slightly different form than for an individual. The easiest way to understand how group egos interact with one another, and how group egos are destroyed (actively or passively – again, there are always these two paths), is by examining some historical examples of group ego. Remember, we are looking at each of these examples not through the lens of social psychology or politics or even through the lens of an historian. Rather, we are attempting to discern how tensions between different group egos play out, and how they are resolved.

In our theory of ego lowering, there are no judgments about right or wrong ways to lower the ego – there are simply passive ways, which are painful but unconscious, and active ways, which are conscious and much less painful (although rarely pain*less*). Just as no individual can be held responsible for lowering another person's ego (as this would be a contradiction to the axiom that says we must drop our belief in our own victimization), no group ego can be responsible for lowering another group's ego. Rather, each group attracts to itself the circumstances it needs in order to lower its own ego, just as each individual does. If one group ego is lowered as a result of action taken by another group, it's not necessarily because the other group had any greater wisdom. We must recognize that in terms of ego dynamics, there is an impersonal quality to group ego interactions. Conflicts arise between groups of different ego zones, and it is the progression of the conflicts that eventually bring the egos into closer balance, thus finding a new level of harmony. Let us see how this has worked in the past.

EIGHTEEN

The French Revolution

The group ego of France as a country was 45% in 1789. At first glance, this does not seem extraordinarily high so we might wonder why the country would need to go through the bloodshed that it was about to experience. Let's dig a little deeper.

The country was sharply divided between the aristocracy (which included the King, the nobility, and the Catholic Church hierarchy on one side), and the people (the bourgeoisie and the peasantry) on the other. The group ego of the people of France in 1789 was 45%. But the group ego of the aristocracy was different – it was 99%. Clearly, the aristocracy was out of alignment with both the country and the people and a re-balancing was needed.

There was ample reason for the people of France not only to distrust their rulers, but also to actively resent them. The aristocracy was oblivious to the plight of the people, which they held in contempt. The aristocrats flounced around, obsessed with balls and costumes and petty intrigues, spending vast sums of money taxed from the labor of the people on monuments to their vanity. Meanwhile, the people were fully aware of the attitude of contempt with which their rulers regarded them, and this bred enormous resentment.

One of the men who came along to lead the revolution was himself a New Soul – a 100% ego figure. Robespierre was able to rally the people to take charge of their country and do away with the corrupt monarchy. In the process, however, he brought the rest of the country's ego with him. France's national ego under Robespierre's leadership inflated to 100% at the height of the Revolutionary Terror. There is, as you will remember, only one way to lower an ego from 100%: death.

Death certainly came. Not only for the thousands that lost their heads to "Mme. La Guillotine," (which ultimately included Robespierre and most of the Revolutionary leadership) but for the entire system of governance as well, which was replaced by an imperial system under Napoleon - another 100% ego.

The turmoil did not end until the fall of Napoleon. By that time the aristocracy, the bourgeoisie, and France's national ego were all back in balance at 45%. But there is an interesting detail to note: the group ego of France's aristocracy actually was humbled and had dropped to 45% early on, after King Louis XVI and Queen Marie Antoinette as well as scores of noble men and women and clergy were beheaded. Why, then, did the Revolution continue, claiming so many thousands of lives?

The answer is because although the aristocracy was now in balance with the country, the bourgeoisie (the new ruling class) was now *out* of balance. Having followed 100% leaders such as Robespierre and Napoleon, and now thirsty for power and conquest, the group ego of the bourgeoisie ballooned until the group ego of the entire country was at 100%, which was why the unrest had to continue until it came back into balance. This finally came to pass at the conclusion of the Napoleonic Wars, which claimed hundreds of thousands of lives. So it was not until France was crushed and Napoleon lost power that the entire process was completed, and a newly humbled France was back in balance.

Now let's look at something even more interesting: an alternate path of history. Was there a better path? Let's say, a path of "Conscious Self-Transformation" for France's group ego? Perhaps there was. Had the French people not followed Robespierre and his ilk but instead instituted a very simple program of non-cooperation with the aristocracy, the same end would have been accomplished, but with far less death of individuals.

The aristocracy in France was removed from the people, yet it depended on them for its very survival, being essentially a parasitic class. Had the bourgeoisie and the peasantry simply colluded in being unwilling to cooperate with the aristocracy, the monarchy would have fallen almost immediately for it had no real power – it depended on the people it ruled over to supply it. With their supply lines cut off, the aristocratic hold on power would have been broken, their humbled group ego would have dropped, and the country would have come back into balance. The only thing this plan required that the French did not have were wise (i.e. lower ego) leaders to make it happen, as it is a strategy that 100% ego leaders could never be capable of implementing. But there is another situation, a true historical case, where such a thing did happen. Let us take a look at British-ruled India.

NINETEEN

India's Independence

The situation in colonial India was strikingly similar to the situation in pre-revolutionary France. In this case, the native Indian population group ego was 45%, while the group ego of the British was 99%, another situation where clearly, an imbalance existed that needed correction.

Fortunately for the Indians, they had a leader who saw that it was not necessary to have a bloody and violent revolution. Gandhi led the people of India through a peaceful program of non-cooperation with the British. Of course, at times the people got carried away with zeal, but the overall method was one of non-violence, and it worked. The British found they were unable to function as rulers without the consent and cooperation of those they governed, and they left India.

However, like in France, something strange happened at this point. The process did not end here, but continued on, and this time, it was bloody. The partition between the Hindus and Muslims resulted in a war, the creation of the independent state of Pakistan, and the relocation of millions of people. No one knows for sure how many on every side – Hindu, Muslim, Sikh – died, but we know it was perhaps in the millions, on all sides. Why did this have to occur?

According to our testing, the ego of the Hindu population at the time India achieved its independence was 60%, while the ego of the Muslim population was 45% (apparently, something akin to what happened with the people of France happened here, which is that in victory, some egos went up). Clearly, these two groups were distinct from one another. Such an imbalance between the two dominant groups in India had to be resolved, and this time those group egos took the Path of Pain and Suffering. It was in fact a passive path, because they were completely unaware of the true principles at work in the conflict. When they had taken the Path of Conscious Transformation, following Gandhi, his followers were aware of the underlying principle at work: no one can rule without the consent of the governed. They were consciously invoking that principle, and restraining any unnecessary force. As a result, the effects were relatively immediate, and relatively peaceful.

When the partition occurred, it happened because the egos of the two groups needed to come into balance. Unfortunately, it was more difficult for them to put their principles into practice with their own countrymen. Passions ran higher, and the results spoke for themselves. They lowered their egos and came into balance, but they did it the hard way.

TWENTY

World War II

Now let's talk about another conflict, one which touched the lives of even more people, and one whose repercussions continue to ripple out: World War II.

So far our examples have been limited to civil unrest within a country, but this example is different. This example deals explicitly with conflict between nations and ideologies, as well as issues of persecution based on religion, ethnicity, sexual orientation and disabilities. Touchy subjects, and even today the debate remains open on whether it was morally correct to drop the atomic bomb to end the war with Japan. In our examination of this subject we are not looking to establish morality so much as seeking to understand the nature of how group egos interact with one another and how they are diminished.

In all of our research on past wars, we have found there is always an aggressor and a defender, and the aggressor's actions always, *always* register at 100% on the ego scale. This is without exception. The responder's actions always register as neutral (0%) on the ego scale. This revelation is of tremendous importance.

The implication is that it is never supportable to be the aggressor in a conflict. Even if a party has a legitimate complaint, there is only one correct course of action: non-engagement with the offender. This can be supplemented with attempts at diplomacy and containment, but it must never be superseded by attack. On the opposite side we have those put in the position of defending themselves, and it turns out that defense is always justified – so long as it is defense. A defender's response to an aggressor's attack always rates at (0) on the ego power scale, which means that it is a neutral action.

There is no such thing as a righteous war. There is simply this interplay between aggressor, whose actions rate at 100% ego, and responder, whose actions neutralize the actions of the aggressor. Neither side can claim righteousness.

Sometimes, defense transforms into offense, and at that time, the actions are no longer justified. When defenders become offenders, their actions rate as 100% ego actions. A good example of this is the policy of ethnic cleansing, mass rape, and collective punishment of the defenseless German population that the Soviets perpetrated after the war had ended and Germany had unconditionally surrendered.

Now let's move on to some of the particulars of this war, including the group ego measures of the different groups at play. The overall group ego of the democracies of Western Europe before WWII was in the High Ego Zone at 75%, as were Britain's and France's respective national egos. We know from our studies of individuals that when you're in the High Ego Zone and you take the passive path, you're in for some trouble, and it will usually be 100% egos that will deliver it to you. Sure enough, Japan's group ego when it started the war in Asia was 100%, as was Germany's and the USSR's when they invaded and divided up Poland (whose ego was at 97%).

It is interesting to note that Germany's group ego when Hitler came to power in 1933 was at 90%. As you can see, under Hitler's insane leadership (need we say that he was at 100% ego himself?) the group ego of the whole country went up to 100%. This is much like the group ego of France under the leadership of Robespierre and Napoleon during the Revolution. Likewise, the group ego of Russia under Lenin and Stalin's equally destructive leadership was also 100% (both were 100% egos). There is clearly a pattern.

If you remember, the only way an ego at 100% drops is death. In the case of group ego, it's not necessarily the deaths of the individuals of that group – *it is the death of the group ego structure.* It is possible that the death of the group ego could involve a peaceful dissolution. This is what ultimately happened at the end of the Cold War, when the Soviet Union finally collapsed - its group ego dropped down to 74% (the medium ego zone) in 1991, and the whole Communist regime collapsed after nearly 75 years of absolute control. But in 1945 for Germany and Japan, there was no chance of such a peaceful dissolution, because their group egos were still at 100%. Neither group ego was affected or diminished by the events of the war – until the group ego structure was completely destroyed – because the only way a 100% ego is reduced is through death. For a 100% ego there is no incremental change, there is only complete annihilation and then re-birth.

Since it was necessary for Japan's 100% group ego to die in order for Japan to progress, the act of dropping the atomic bomb on Hiroshima and Nagasaki rates as a 0 on the ego scale – a neutral act in response to aggression.

Keep in mind again that we are merely looking at the ego scale and group ego dynamics and searching for examples of how such dynamics manifest in the real world. Remember that in this context, actions are not rated as right or wrong, they are rated on the ego scale. Death for a 100% ego is a neutralizing act. However, let us not make the error of attempting to extrapolate from the group level to the individual level. Just because the action of the group ego rates as 0% (neutral) on the ego scale does NOT mean that the egos of the individuals in that group are at 0%, nor can we make any assumptions about their motivations or intentions. We only know that viewed in the context of group ego interactions, neutral is where this action rated. Again, we have aggressors and defenders, actors and responders, and they do a universal, impersonal dance with one another until they come into a level of harmony and balance that quiets the conflicts.

Both Germany and Japan dropped from 100% to 74%, just out of the high ego zone, when they were crushed and surrendered unconditionally. For each of these countries, their surrender was more than just giving up in a war; it was the death of a whole regime, or rather, the death of that group ego structure. You will notice that both countries went on from this point to rebuild themselves in stunning new ways, and this is no coincidence. They simply could not have become the successful, peaceful countries they are now had they not dropped their pathological egos and been re-born.

By the end of WWII the collective ego of war-torn Western Europe had dropped more than 30 points from 75% down to 44%, into the low ego zone. Remember that one definition of ego is separation, and it is at this point in European history (after thousands of years of almost nonstop warfare and bloodshed) that for the first time ever all these nations dropped their atavistic antagonism and started a process of unification and peaceful coexistence. WWI and WWII were the processes of ego destruction that brought Western Europe down from high to low ego.

TWENTY-ONE

Individual Ego Interacting With Group Ego - The Dilemma

We humans often wonder if war is necessary, or why we experience genocides, natural disasters, plagues or other catastrophes. Why are these experiences inflicted on certain groups at certain times? The answer is an interesting one: group ego challenges and conflicts arise as an opportunity for the individual members of the group(s) involved to drop their egos. These conflicts are "ego lowering" vehicles. Therefore, the appropriate course of action for an individual in response to a group ego challenge or conflict depends on the individual's ego level.

In our research, we looked extensively into the correct action for an individual of various ego zones when interacting with a group ego. The most interesting and complicated choices always arise when there is a conflict between two or more group egos, such as in war. It turns out the correct choice for an individual is dependent upon two factors: the first factor is whether the individual's ego score is 45% or above (high to medium ego zone), or below 45%(low ego zone). Individuals with egos below 45% should never participate in any group ego conflicts, no matter what the position of their group is. Once you are in the low ego zone, it is your job to refrain from playing a part in those dramas whose main purpose is to lower individual egos on a mass scale.

The second factor is the moral position of the group to whom the individual belongs. If the group is engaging in offensive action, such as Japan's aggression in WWII, the individual should not cooperate with it, no matter what the individual's ego score is. But if the group's action is a neutral response, then how the individual responds is different if the individual's ego is above or below 45%.

Let's start with the scenario of an individual whose country's offensive action is at 100%. The correct course of action for this individual is to not engage with the actions of the group. In this case, the appropriate choice is non-participation. Generally, the best way to not participate is to go into exile. If exile is impossible the next best course of action is to hide out within one's own country, avoiding the conflict and any participation in it.

Now let's take a different scenario. Imagine someone whose ego is above 45% and whose country is invaded by another country. Clearly, his country is the responder, which means his country's self-defensive action rates at 0, or neutral. This person should help in the defensive war effort. Since there is no better opportunity to lower your ego than to participate in fighting a war, this is the time when one should volunteer, and go out and fight.

Let's look at one last scenario. Imagine a country that is not physically invaded, but is nevertheless responding to the aggressive actions of another party by either defending itself or helping to defend someone else. In this case, the country's actions are still neutral, because it is supporting a responder cause in a conflict. But individuals of this country should not sign up and fight. Neither should they protest the war, as their country's actions are neutralizing the aggression. Instead, they should fight if called upon to fight (i.e. a draft) and otherwise go about their business, neither avoiding the conflict nor going out of their way to participate in it.

An interesting example of this third scenario is the American Civil War. Although whether the South had the right to secede is still disputed, what is not disputed is that the Confederate Army fired the first shot when it bombed Fort Sumter. This made the South the aggressor in the conflict (actions = 100% ego), and the North the responder (actions = 0 ego, or neutral). The North then invaded the South. Twice the South tried to invade the North but was defeated both times, so the North was never invaded. This is important, because if the North had been invaded, the correct action for a Northern man with an ego above 45% would have been to sign up and volunteer to fight. As it was, the moral action for a Southern man of any ego zone was to avoid the conflict by going into exile or hiding, while the moral action for a Northern man above 45% was to serve only if drafted, and for a Northern man below 45% was to avoid the conflict entirely, even if drafted.

To illustrate how an individual's ego may be affected through engagement with group ego, here is a true-life story of three American brothers who came of age during the Vietnam War. All three had egos in the high ego zone.

The U.S. position in Vietnam was neutral, as it was supporting a responder party, South Vietnam, which was responding to North Vietnamese aggression.

The oldest brother was drafted, but instead of serving, fled to Canada. The middle brother, anticipating the draft, signed up and was shipped to Vietnam where he was assigned a desk job and never had to go into combat. (Note: in this case, his actions rate the same on the ego scale as if he were drafted, since the step he took to sign up was merely in recognition of the inevitable). The youngest brother was never drafted, nor did he sign up.

So what was the effect on each of the egos of the three brothers? The ego of the oldest brother went down 12 points, since going to Canada was a form of exile, and it caused some humiliation and other kinds of suffering as well. When he returned to the

U.S., he had to undergo a trial as a draft-evader, and his ego dropped another 5 points, still in the high ego zone. In contrast, the ego of the middle brother dropped twenty-five points as a result of going to war and he came back with his ego now in the middle ego zone. The ego of the youngest brother didn't change at all.

In summary, the oldest brother avoided the call of duty and although his ego dropped, it did not drop as much as it could have and it remained in the high ego zone. The second brother did do precisely as he was supposed to, so he got the full benefit of the opportunity that was presented to him. The youngest brother also took correct action: he neither avoided fighting nor was he drafted. For whatever reason, this was not his path to ego lowering.

The story doesn't end there, of course. If we miss an opportunity, there will always be others, and even if we take an opportunity, we may waste it later. The middle brother, although he dropped his ego twenty-five points when he went to Vietnam, raised it back again quite quickly as a result of a substance abuse habit he picked up while he was there. The oldest brother's ego also went back up to where it was after he survived his trial without punishment. His personal life theme of "ego rising" was anger, which led him to give up all that he had gained. The lesson of this real-life story is clear: opportunities (in the form of group ego conflict) are continually presented to lower the ego further, and even once the ego is lower, constant vigilance is required.

TWENTY-TWO

How Individuals Cease to Be Involved in Group Ego Conflicts

As you can see, group ego conflicts are really just mass vehicles for individuals to lower their egos, so if the ego is already low, there is no need to become involved. In fact, the only way to cease to be involved with group ego conflicts is to enter the low ego zone. Once there, it is the duty of those with low egos to recognize the eternal dance that is at play in each of these conflicts, and to hold a consciousness of non-judgment for those who do become involved through their identification with one position or another and their subsequent desire to see that position win. This may be a subtle identification – nothing more than a belief in the person's heart, yet, it still denotes an attachment to the outcome, and thus will create suffering on the part of that person.

Those with low ego can remember that the individuals participating are merely taking the perfect opportunity to drop their egos, which takes courage. Low-ego people can recognize this, and can have compassion for the heartache and suffering of those involved while simultaneously resisting the temptation to attach to one position or another. This principle applies to any group ego conflict – whether it is during a violent episode such as war, or during peacetime when partisan political conflicts tend to take center stage. It even applies to what we think of as silly things – for instance, becoming so identified with your alma mater that you live and die with their football team. To do so is still to engage with group ego, and you will (eventually) suffer as a result.

An easy way to test your ego position on any group conflict is to take a moment and feel your inner response to each of the parties involved. If anything other than compassion arises towards any party, *you have already attached yourself to a position in the conflict, and are therefore a part of it.* If you have the urge to argue over which side is right or wrong in the conflict, rather than calmly discuss the morality of certain actions, you are attached to a position in the conflict and are a part of it. To be a part of the conflict means that you will suffer with the group with which you are identifying. To remove yourself from the conflict and view all sides with compassion means to remove yourself from group suffering.

As you can see, although group egos are an extension of individual egos, they are more complex, and less controllable by the individual. The only way to control our involvement in group ego conflicts is to lower our individual egos to the point where we no longer need or desire to take part in such conflicts,. Thus, the solution to the problem of group ego conflict is precisely the same as the solution to the problem of individual ego: neutralize your own ego. Take the active path and bring your ego to the lowest level you possibly can. This will translate into not only a changed perspective on life and the events that take place in it, but into less suffering on your part and a greater ability to support your fellow human beings in love and compassion – *all* your fellow human beings.

TWENTY-THREE

What Happens When We Overcome the Ego... and What Do We Do Next?

We have not yet spoken of the joy that arises in the peaceful space we enter when we have resisted the pull of the ego, even if it is only a momentary victory. It happens in the little moments, when instead of making an angry accusation we take a deep breath and pause, remembering that any time we are tempted to engage in a struggle with someone or something outside of ourselves, it is nothing more than a temptation of the ego.

When we resist the urge to follow our egos, we have the ability to no longer get emotionally wrapped up in the events of group ego. Instead, we can recognize them as ego-lowering opportunities. Rather than becoming passionate, we can choose to tune in to the silence inside and recognize that this is merely a temptation to choose sides, to believe that one side is wrong and the other is right. This temptation will always lead us astray if we give in to it. Perhaps it is a case of war - even then, there is no good and bad: there is simply aggressor and responder. Each is playing its part in this group ego drama that was created through group ego consciousness to give opportunities to individuals in each group to lower their egos. In such cases, each individual will have a role to play, but the more we drop our egos the more we will be able to see that we never need to work "against" anyone or anything, for there is nothing outside of our own selves to work against.

When we have overcome the pull of our ego, even for a moment, we understand that it is our own ego that is our only enemy. In this recognition we are able to stop railing against the injustice of life or other people and start engaging in true contemplation of the right course of action in our present circumstances, whatever they may be.

The eternal truth is this: *all conditions reflect the activity of the consciousness of the individuals concerned.* The conditions we experience in life are thus an outward expression of what is going on inside of us, and this is true for everyone concerned in the circumstance. We are never the victims of other people or of circumstances, rather we are constantly experiencing outer conditions that reflect our inner state. When we have overcome the ego, whether it is a momentary victory or the final one, we are able to realize this truth, deep in our most sacred selves. We have the capacity to no longer see the negativity we encounter in our circumstances as separate and apart from ourselves, as a condition or circumstance with which must struggle. Instead we may remember, "peace, be still," and let the condition go by returning to the source of peace inside ourselves. The moment we change our inner state by ceasing to listen and obey the voice of the ego, the outer condition shifts, because a change of consciousness has occurred. Even if the outer picture appears not to have changed, our experience of it shifts immediately, and that is the key point.

Yet, destroying our ego is only one half of the work to arrive at a state of Truth. The other half of our work involves opening our hearts and actively developing our capacity to love. We call this process *building soulfulness*.

III. SOULFULNESS

TWENTY-FOUR

Phil

Phil was a TV weather forecaster with a 99% ego and zero soulfulness. He was relatively successful in his profession and had earned a degree of local notoriety, but he was sarcastic, unfriendly, and sometimes downright nasty in the way he treated others. He did not have any friends or a close relationship, although he did have some fans.

Due to a snowstorm one day, Phil got stuck in a small town called Punxsutawney, where the local citizens were throwing a huge celebration in honor of Groundhog Day. Despite the fact he was trapped in Punxsutawney for the day and had nowhere else to go and nothing better to do, he refused to join in the celebration. He sneered and scowled at the festivities and those who were enjoying them, whom he called "hicks." Phil was clearly a very unhappy person who masked his unhappiness (even from himself) with scorn.

If you have seen the movie *Groundhog Day*[5], you know what happens next. Phil finds himself in a loop, endlessly repeating the same day – Groundhog Day - in the small town of Punxsutawney. Each day he wakes up and although he remembers the previous day, no one else does. He is starting the same day all over again, and he can live it however he likes. Although this is initially confusing, once he gets past the strangeness of it, he embarks on a journey of self transformation that exactly parallels the route many of us take in consciousness, in particular as we lower our egos and increase our soulfulness.

The first thing Phil does when he realizes that he will always wake up in Punxsutawney on Groundhog Day exactly the same as the day before is indulge all his most negative desires and habits. He eats like a pig. He uses information he gathers about the women in the town to seduce them. Knowing there will be no consequences for his

---

[5] Ramis, H (Director), Albert, T (Producer) & Rubin, D., Ramis, H. (Writers). (2008), *Groundhog Day* [DVD], United States: Sony Pictures Home Entertainment (Original release date 1993).

actions since he will wake up the next morning and everything will be right back where it was, he steals money, drinks too much (he won't have a hangover the next morning) and basically does whatever he wants without any regard for other people.

Eventually, this becomes boring to him, and he realizes he is unfulfilled and restless. He decides to set his sights higher and use his advantage to get his producer, Rita (the woman he really wants) to fall in love with him under false pretenses. That is, he uses the fact that he knows he will have plenty of times to re-live the same day to get information from Rita that will make it seem to her, the next day, that he sees into her soul. But what he is really doing is manipulating the situation, trying to change her perception of him, rather than investing in true inner change. He is, in ego terms, projecting his problem outside of himself and engaging in a struggle to change those around him, which is a high-ego zone approach to life.

After he fails miserably at this he takes a self-destructive detour down Self Pity Lane and decides to enjoy killing himself in any way he can just to prove his superiority (he knows he'll still wake up the next morning, just as he always does, on Groundhog Day). This phase ends when he not only becomes bored of it, but he realizes it simply isn't getting him what he wants any more than his previous strategy did.

At last, Phil begins to engage in the process of inner transformation. At this point, his ego is in the low ego zone, having been beaten out of him not only through his repeated embarrassing failures but by his numerous deaths. His low ego is apparent because he is interacting with people differently. For instance, he is real and honest with Rita about what is happening to him, even though he knows she will think he is crazy. There is definitely something different about him, and he really isn't so offensive anymore. What Phil is still lacking, however, is a degree of soulfulness. He has dropped the mask he was wearing but he still isn't truly happy or fulfilled.

This is the state of a person who has arrived at a state of Grace but not a state of Love.

When we want to win love, we must first give love. Phil has lowered his ego – now he needs to open his heart and grow his capacity to love. He finds himself suddenly motivated to help others so he looks around for someone to help and the first person he notices is the old man on the corner begging for change – the man he has passed by every day in Punxsutawney. For the first time, he reaches into his pocket and gives him money. Then he takes him out to eat and gets him cleaned up. Tragically, the old man still dies at the end of the day, and Phil realizes just how short and precious life is.

As Phil's soulfulness grows, he begins to notice the other people in town and starts to step in to help them wherever he can. For instance, every day he makes sure to be under the tree where a child falls and catches him before he hits the ground. The child never thanks him, but instead runs off to continue playing with his friends. Nevertheless, Phil is always there.

He notices that three older women always have an issue with a flat tire, so he starts showing up right in time to fix it. He becomes interested and involved in the lives of the people of the town and listens to their stories, sometimes offering advice, other times helping them celebrate happy occasions. He does all of this every day, over and over.

Interestingly, as Phil focuses more and more on his inner transformation and building what we call *soulfulness* (his capacity for love), he doesn't forget about Rita or his love for her, but he does stop obsessing about her. When he finally and at last wins her love, it is true love for the person he has become, not love for a false image of him. More importantly, by this time, Phil's soulfulness is so developed that not only does he love, respect and feel comfortable with himself, but his heart has expanded to include virtually every individual in the small town of Punxsutawney. What did this bring him? *Phil was happy.*

He wasn't any more financially successful than he was on the very first Groundhog Day. He wasn't any more professionally accomplished (although he did perfect some skills, like playing piano and ice sculpture, along the way). He wasn't more powerful and he didn't own any more worldly goods. In fact, not one single exterior factor about Phil had changed. *The only thing that had changed was Phil,* and the most important part of that change was that he had become amazingly soulful and therefore was living every day steeped in the love of those around him as well as the love of his own heart. Dropping his ego in the low ego zone allowed him to finally make the right priorities: love first. The rest will take care of itself.

TWENTY-FIVE

What Is Soulfulness?

Soulfulness is what many people think of as "positive ego." Again, our definition of the ego does not conform to Freud's, for what we call the "ego" is probably closer to what he termed the "id." So let us be clear: according to our definition of ego, there is no such thing as "positive ego." Ego is synonymous with negativity, a belief that we are separate from our Source and each other. Soulfulness, on the other hand, is our ability to express and receive love.

It is important to recognize that the absence of ego does not guarantee the presence of love. Love exists in interaction, whether it is with ourselves or with another person(s). It is necessary to cultivate love in order to become an expression of love. Love does not arise passively. We call this cultivation of love *soulfulness*, which is the active opposite of ego. This is the other half of the goal of attaining a state of Truth: to become Love incarnate. Unlike with the ego, however, there is no passive, default way to build soulfulness. The only way is the active way.

As you might expect by now, there are a number of different ways of building soulfulness – fourteen, to be exact. It's not necessary to practice them all (although we would never discourage anyone from trying!) The ones you naturally love to do, you will do anyway. So it's only necessary to choose the ones you have the most resistance to, the ones you are most reluctant to do, and practice those. In that way, you'll be lowering your ego by overcoming your resistance, and building your soulfulness at the same time! What could be better?

Let's take a look at the list on the next page. One of the first things we noticed in our research was that people who were part of a larger group or community of some kind tend to have a higher soulfulness score, regardless of their ego scores. Of course, an ego in the very High Ego Zone (100%) would prevent a person from having a significantly high soulfulness score, but once the ego drops below 100%, an individual is capable of building his soulfulness to the highest level possible.

To Build Soulfulness

1. Build community
   (connect with others in a consistent fashion)

2. Support others
   (emotional support and guidance or mentorship)

3. Practice non-defensiveness

4. Educate and learn with others

5. Honor others

6. Cooperate with others

7. Share with others
   (specifically time and money)

8. Provide for others
   (assistance and material needs)

9. Feed others
   (yes, this is its own category, and yes, it is
   that simple)

10. Play with others
    (games, sports activities, general silliness and
    diversion)

11. Celebrate with others
    (join in celebrations or throw them yourself)

12. Share physical affection with others
    (hugs, holding hands, pats on the back)

13. Practice Gratitude

14. Love others

TWENTY-SIX

The Soulfulness Scale

Before we continue our discussion of soulfulness, we should explain that the scale we use to measure it is different from the ego scale. It's a positive scale, going from 0 (none) to 100 (divine).

A score of 75 is out of reach for all but the most extraordinary human beings. Mother Theresa, for instance, had a score of 70. For most of us the highest we may aspire to is a score of 60, and that is very high indeed.

Low Soulfulness: 0-30

Let's start at the bottom of the scale: someone with a soulfulness score of 0 loves no one, not even herself. A person with a score of 5 may love her dog or cat or pet fish, and perhaps her child if she has one, and that is all. For example, apparently Hitler loved his dogs and maybe his wife, and his score was at 5. That's not to say that everyone who has a soulfulness score of 5 should be compared to Adolf Hitler – we must remember that he also had an ego score of 100%, and what an ego it was! No, this example is simply meant to illustrate that even a psychopathic mass murderer was capable of loving his dogs and his wife, and that is basically what a score of 5 indicates: you love something, but not much.

A score of 10 or 15 is the average person who loves his immediate family and perhaps a couple of friends. This person is not very involved in a community such as a religious organization, non-profit organization, or other community activity. He mostly keeps to himself and his small, built-in community (such as immediate family) and that is all. He is unlikely to be very playful, to celebrate much, or to do many of the other activities on the soulfulness list, although he may occasionally participate in one or two of them.

A score of 20-30 indicates the start of caring involvement in a wider community around the individual: coaching a sports team, volunteering at a homeless shelter or a nursing home, working with children, veterans, or disabled citizens. There are many, many ways this person could be involved in helping others. This person is starting to become involved in supporting a wider community, although she is not fully devoted to it yet.

Middle Soulfulness: 30-40

There isn't much "middle ground" when it comes to soulfulness. Someone with a score between 30-40 is probably on their way to greater soulfulness and is just ramping up to get there. This period merely indicates progressively greater levels of loving involvement in a wider community.

High Soulfulness: 40-60

A score of 40 is an indication that this individual has begun to achieve a successful level of soulfulness. This person is preparing or perhaps beginning to be a leader in one way or another in some sort of soulful work, even if not in an official capacity. Other people may begin to look at this person as an example of how to be soulful.

A score of 50 means that this person is becoming so soulful that his influence is beginning to extend even beyond his local community. He may be a leader at a national level in one of the sort of activities or communities already described, or he may be starting his own soulful organization, and in that case, he has the capacity to sustain that soulful energy for the entire organization.

A score of 60 means that this person's influence is felt and recognized on a large scale. Whatever work this person is doing, and it is most likely as a leader of some sort, is recognized and admired by people far and wide. This person is creating a soulful impact on the world.

There is an elderly couple who have both been our clients for some time. Although they are both in their seventies, they continue to stay active in the large real estate business that they built over the course of their lives. They employ many people. For a long time before we began this line of research, everyone in our office had commented on the sunshine that seemed to fill the office when these two would come in for their regular checkups. They just seem to radiate love. When we tested them on the soulfulness scale we found out why: the husband's soulfulness was at 60, and the wife's was at 50. Incidentally, her ego was at 10, and his was in the low ego zone as well.

This couple is not leading a church or an ashram or any sort of "organized" spiritual activity, but they are certainly leaders. As employers and landlords, they are very involved in the welfare of their employees as well as their tenants. They work tirelessly to give to this community as well as to their family, many of whom live very close by. Often when they come in for their appointments they bring fresh fruit from their fruit trees, or flowers from their garden, for our whole office to enjoy. They remember all our staffers' names as well as the names of their husbands, wives, and children. Although we only see them every six months, they know what is happening in our lives and are sure to check in to see how we are. This is what it means to have high soulfulness.

Very High Soulfulness: 60-100

This brings us to those scores above 60. These scores are special indeed. A person who achieves a soulfulness score of over 60 affects global human consciousness, and transforms it through his understanding and demonstration. This person is such a loving force that even people who have never heard of him, or who have never been directly influenced by him, are indirectly influenced as a result of his actions. He is literally bringing soulfulness to a higher spiritual level, and in so doing, he is advancing global human consciousness.

While it is possible to reach a soulfulness level of 100, we do not know of anyone alive today that is currently above 75, and such people are generally considered saints (i.e. Mother Theresa, at 70).

TWENTY-SEVEN

Building Soulfulness Is Harder Than it Looks

When we first considered the concept of building soulfulness, it seemed to us that it would be easier and more fun to do than to destroy our egos. After all, who doesn't want to be more playful, or celebrate more, or have more joy? How hard can it be to hug more people every day, or to feed others? It turns out, however, that building soulfulness is more difficult for some people than active ego destroying.

Let's look, for example, at the former professional soccer player-turned-surfer that came to us because he was suffering from what can only be termed misery. What we discovered was that his ego was in the low ego zone, but the misery he was experiencing was because he was neither playing soccer, nor coaching soccer, nor getting out and surfing, despite the fact that he lived only 2 blocks from the ocean. What was the number one thing he needed to increase his soulfulness? Playfulness. Yet, he wasn't playing.

Why not? Well, the same reason most of us don't play: he was working. He felt guilty when he took time away from his marriage or his work to play. He felt he should be more successful before he started to play. But since playfulness was integral to his ability to build his soulfulness, he would never reach the success he strove for until he became more playful.

This concept is contradictory to what most of us believe about success. We tend to believe that success is achieved by working hard and striving and sacrificing until one day we attain a pinnacle. Yet if we examine the people that we truly love as a society, we find they are not hardened people who are embittered by spending their lives striving for achievement. No, they are loving, soulful, joyful people. They seem to attract success for their endeavors like magnets – it comes to them at least partly because they are so attractive to people. We admire people who are financially successful, but that cannot be compared to the love we hold for people who are highly soulful.

Now, having a low ego makes us more attractive in a very quiet way, because it brings us to greater peace. This makes us more comfortable for others to be around. Yet that is not the same as being soulful. Soulfulness brings us love and fulfillment. This kind of love brings opportunities for connection and healing that are heartwarming, joyous and meaningful. Being successfully soulful means that we make a true, loving impact on the lives of others in a way that neither they nor we will ever forget.

The famous book series, Chicken Soup for the Soul ® by Jack Canfield and Mark Victor Hansen, is about people who found themselves the recipients of soulfulness, or who discovered new levels of soulfulness inside themselves. Upon reading this collection of stories the inevitable feeling the reader is left with is, *this* is what life (and love) is really all about! Love is playful, it is joyful, it is celebratory, and it only truly exists where it is actually in expression. Love is not a concept; it is active, it is alive. When we tell someone we love him, it means very little. When we *share an expression* of love with someone, it can change our life and theirs.

So this former soccer player had a low ego but he also had very little expression of love in his life. This was the source of his suffering, and the root cause of his lack of success. He needed to play and love more, not work more.

If we are honest with ourselves, most of us think of the things that are included in soulfulness as the "extra" things in life – the happy things that we do if we have the time, the resources and the energy. They are the things that we promise ourselves and others we will do once we are successful. We think of them as rewards for hard work. But this is a backwards way of thinking. In fact, these activities are a calling of the soul and they require every bit as much discipline as the process of actively lowering one's ego. Most importantly they must be done *now*, because they are what make us successful. We have our priorities out of order. Soulfulness is not the reward of success; *success is the reward of soulfulness.*

That is not to say that soulful activities are not enjoyable - they are. But they are not easy. They require us to stretch ourselves open, to take a moment to drop our self-importance and simply be. We must leave behind our emotional armoring and guardedness and connect with other souls in a compassionate, loving, joyful, non-judgmental and accepting manner. We must open our hearts, set aside time in our schedules, and think of others before we think of ourselves. Let's not fool ourselves – this isn't easy for most of us. This is precisely why so many people get depressed at the prospect of family gatherings or holiday celebrations. How many movies are released almost every holiday season where the plot is based on the idea that people dread going home for the holidays to face their "dysfunctional" families? Most of us don't want to practice these activities with our families – we would rather keep judging them and reacting to them the way we always have.

TWENTY-EIGHT

How Does Soulfulness Help ME?

When you think about it, this is a perfectly natural question: "I want to achieve my goals of living a happy life, which you said were perfectly reasonable. So how do all the things on the soulfulness list help me get there? Hugging people? Feeding people? Providing for others?"

"Not that these aren't nice things," we would all hastily add, if we were really having this conversation. "It's just that, while they are nice things to do, it's hard to see how they will help me achieve my goals."

It's a fair question. Although the teaching that "it is better to give than to receive" or "do unto others as you would have them do unto you" is common, we can't take it for granted. Again, we ask the question: WHY?

To answer that question, let's revisit Phil in *Groundhog Day*.

As we observe how happy Phil is at the end of the movie compared to how miserable he was at the beginning, we notice something significant: Phil was the same person, living the same day, in the same place, with all of the same resources, on the last day as he was on the first. All the love and enjoyment that he found on the last day was there, completely available to him, the very first morning that he awoke in Punxsutawney on Groundhog Day. The only difference between the first and last day and every other day in between was that on the last day, Phil saw the town, its inhabitants, and himself differently. He saw opportunities for love and caring and connection that he did not see the first day, although they were all around him, completely available to him. The only thing, in short, that had changed, was Phil: he had lowered his ego into the low ego zone, and he had grown his soulfulness to a high level. Phil was at last happy to be himself, to be where he was, doing whatever was there for him to do from that loving place inside his own heart.

So you see, building soulfulness is what the Unknown Confederate soldier was talking about in his famous poem, *The Blessing of Unanswered Prayers*, when he stated,

> I asked for strength that I might achieve,
> I was made weak that I might learn humbly to obey.
> I asked for health that I might do greater things,
> I was given infirmity that I might do better things.
> I asked for riches that I might be happy,
> I was given poverty that I might be wise.
> I asked for power that I might have the praise of men
> I was given weakness that I might feel the need of God.
> I asked for all things that I might enjoy life,
> I was given life that I might enjoy all things.
> I got nothing that I had asked for,
> But everything that I had hoped for.
> Almost despite myself my unspoken prayers were answered.
> I am, among all men, most richly blessed

Much of this poem actually describes the process of having one's ego lowered. But the key part - the end - is what deals with building soulfulness: *"I asked for all things that I might enjoy life, I was given life that I might enjoy all things / I got nothing that I had asked for, but everything I had hoped for."* This is a man who has not only been humbled, but who is grateful for the humbling experience. That gratitude is the root of soulfulness.

Our dreams come true when our ego no longer keeps us separate from others and our heart is connected with other hearts – when our deepest desires for love and connection are fulfilled, not when a certain balance is reached in our bank accounts. Note that Phil did get what he wanted most – he got Rita's love. But he only got her love once he found his own true love inside himself, and that was every bit as important; indeed, it was of primary importance. Rita only added to his already soulful state, she didn't create it for him. She couldn't.

That brings us to another excellent and famous example of a man learning soulfulness: Ebenezer Scrooge. *A Christmas Carol* by Charles Dickens (we prefer the movie *Scrooged*, also with Bill Murray, but any version will do) is nothing other than the story of a man who was so focused on his financial success that he completely shut down his heart and forgot to love. At the beginning of the story, Scrooge's soulfulness is at 0. By the very end, it's at 60. There is no more vivid example of what happens when we prioritize attaining success above loving and what we shall reap if we do. This story has resonated with audiences for over a hundred and fifty years for good reason – we all unconsciously recognize the challenge of opening ourselves up to loving activity and we need to be reminded of what shall befall us if we do not, and what rewards await us if we do.

Soulfulness isn't always easy even for those for whom we think it clearly should be. Another client of ours was a young rabbi who had a beautiful wife and five young, adorable children. His life was devoted to a religious pursuit, and he was surrounded by a large extended family and a tight-knit community. Interestingly, he came to see us because of a heart condition. After looking at the physical manifestations of the condition, we sought the underlying spiritual and emotional causes, and what came up was a lack of soulfulness. He needed to play and celebrate more, and because he was not doing those two things, it was affecting his *heart*. Need we say more? We told him to go home, spend more quality time with his loving wife, play with his children, celebrate life, and practice gratitude for all that he had. Everything he needed to do was right in front of him, but he was taking his responsibilities so seriously he was failing to celebrate and be grateful. So often it is the case that we have everything we need, and yet we do not realize it.

Let's go back to those goals that most of us hold: achievement in our professional lives, material abundance, and satisfaction in our family and romantic relationships. We now see that all of these things are possible not through the kind of hard work and competition most of us are trained to expect, but through the challenging but rewarding tasks of relinquishing our egos and opening our hearts. We then realize that everything we ever wanted was right there in front of us, we simply couldn't see past our huge egos to recognize it. As we said at the very beginning of this book, seek the state of Truth first. You will then find that your goals are fulfilled effortlessly and gracefully, and you know now this is because the answers were always there, right in front of you all along.

TWENTY-NINE

How and Why We Get Sick

The story of the rabbi beautifully illustrates the foundational belief of our practice: If we understand that all of life is consciousness unfolding, and that we are here to stretch ourselves to express our divine spiritual potential, we can understand why we have our physical, mental, and emotional "alert system," which is what we think of as disease or dysfunction. We are spiritual beings. Our true essence is nothing but pure consciousness, pure spirit. Our challenge as embodied spirit is to fully and completely express our divine spiritual nature in all of our four dimensions: physical, emotional, mental, and spiritual. When we fall short of this, our bodies get out of balance, and we are alerted to the imbalance by some sort of pain. *ex. night foot - netzach imbalance -*

If we trace the pain back to its physical beginning, we will surely find one, and that is what we have traditionally thought of as the "cause." Yet it is not the true cause but instead merely the physical root, the very beginning of the physical manifestation of the dysfunction, just as the first root of the tree is the very beginning of the physical manifestation of the living tree itself. What is the first thing a seed does when it cracks open and begins to grow? It sends out a root. But is the root the "cause" of the tree? No it is not, it is the first part of the growing tree, and the part from which every other part grows. So what is the cause of the tree? The seed? No indeed. The seed could sit there forever and never sprout. What makes the seed sprout? Well, we could say that the right conditions for the seed to sprout are what makes it sprout – the right soil, sunlight, and water. But are those conditions the "cause" of the tree? No, they are not. They could be there all the time, and without the seed, they would produce nothing.

What, then, "causes" the tree? Life. The tree, like us, is a physical expression of divine spiritual nature. There is no physical "cause" of the tree, there is only a physical *beginning* to the tree. The cause of the tree is the irresistible Life force that flows through all of creation, bringing together the seed with the right conditions for its germination so it may be a physical vessel for Life to express Itself further.

We are just like the tree. There is no physical "cause" to our suffering any more than there is a physical "cause" to our joy. There is simply a physical beginning. Behind that beginning, there is a spiritual animating principle. When our consciousness is in accord with that principle, the result is physical harmony. When our consciousness is out of alignment with that principle, the result is physical discord. The physical discord is not a punishment for bad behavior, it is an alarm system, meant to alert us, to raise our awareness of the state we are in so we can shift appropriately and bring ourselves back into alignment with our spiritual Source.

So, our truest, deepest nature is ego-less and wholly soulful. Completely loving, totally fearless, all positive and no negative. Our true nature is light, and just as light dispels all darkness, as Eleanor Roosevelt said, "There is not enough darkness in all the world to overcome the light from one tiny candle." When we uncover and reveal our own light by destroying our ego and building our soulfulness, we dispel our own darkness and shine forth in our radiant brilliance. Thus, the path of destroying our ego and building our soulfulness gives us much more than physical health and harmony – it gives us a state of Truth. It opens our hearts so we may experience true loving and joyful fulfillment not only within ourselves, but also in our larger communities.

THIRTY

Practical Soulfulness-Building

Let's review the list of soulfulness-building actions: building community, supporting others, non-defensiveness, educating others, honoring others, cooperating with others, sharing with others, providing for others, feeding others, playing with others, celebrating with others, being affectionate with others, practicing gratitude and loving others. Here's the key with each one of these: it only takes one instance of any of these activities to raise your soulfulness at least one point. Again, building soulfulness is simple, even if it isn't always easy to overcome our resistance to doing so.

In addition to the minimum one point raise, keep in mind the greater the effort put forward, the more our soulfulness will build (the more points we will accrue). For instance, if we find it difficult to host a dinner and cook for other people, but easy to play with other people, we'll build more soulfulness by cooking (but that doesn't mean we shouldn't play – of course we should). Ultimately, a truly soulful person can and will perform any of these activities not only without resistance, but with true joy. That is the goal.

What this means is that we can build soulfulness as fast as we want to. It is possible, and we have witnessed this happen with our clients, for people to radically transform themselves in a matter of months. It just takes the effort of choosing an activity and then overcoming our resistance by sticking to it regularly. Anyone can do it, and anyone can get to at least 60 on the soulfulness scale. It's simply a matter of setting the intention, making the activity a priority, then following through. It could take just an extra five minutes out of your day, or it could take more than that, but that is up to you. It doesn't need to be a major undertaking, it just needs to happen, even if only for a moment.

THIRTY-ONE

What Would the World Look Like...

We come now to the goal of all of this ego destroying and soulfulness-building: the state of Truth. This state is defined as a high state of soulfulness (60+) combined with a low ego (35% or less). The state of Truth is reached when a person lives both in a deep state of Grace and in a high state of Love simultaneously. This is a very, very special state that holds tremendous implications not only for the individual herself, but also for the world.

The person who dwells in a state of Truth brings to this earth a gift that is impossible to quantify. This person is full of love combined with almost no ego. This may be the highest state a human being can reach while still living in society. This is our goal.

Now, imagine if we had a society with a critical mass of people who were dwelling in a state of Truth. What would the planet look like then?

In such a low-ego, highly soulful society, every individual would be provided for, fed, honored, and cared for, and everyone would practice cooperating with one another. This society would truly realize and bring into full expression the concept of a single family of mankind, peace on earth and goodwill towards all human beings. This society would express Heaven on Earth by acting through each and every individual.

So what about all the other attempts to create such a society, you may ask. The Communists tried it, and Socialists everywhere are currently trying it. The Christians have been trying for centuries; the hippies tried it. So far as we know right now, none of these attempts have been successful. Human nature is what it is, isn't it? It's never going to change …is it?

The surprising answer to that question is: yes, it will change. It will change not by having that change imposed upon it, such as through a political or religious dictate, or by a messianic olam chesed yibaneh

leader, but by one individual at a time doing the inner work to arrive at a state of Truth. At a specific tipping point, enough people will have reached this state that global human consciousness will change. This is what will bring about true Peace on Earth, or what is often referred to as the Golden Age.

We often meet people whose sole goal is to become enlightened as quickly as possible. These people have experienced so much pain in their lives that they wish to escape the cycle of death and rebirth and cease to be incarnate. We wish to make this clear: the path to the state of Truth is on the way to enlightenment, but it is not enlightenment itself. Furthermore, it is completely possible to achieve enlightenment while bypassing the need to reach such a high state of soulfulness. In other words, achieving a state of Truth is optional, an elective you might say, on the way to graduation. However, and this is the key point - it is not possible to achieve the state of Heaven on Earth unless our society as a whole achieves a state of Truth. Individuals may reach enlightenment on their own and withdraw from society as a result of having done so, but we will never transform the world itself unless a critical mass of individuals (35%) first achieves a state of Truth.

Let's offer an analogy to illustrate: right now, planet Earth is like a giant school for human beings, where we expand our consciousness by learning many things, including how to lower our egos and raise our soulfulness. We graduate from planet Earth once we have achieved enlightenment, which we define as a high state of consciousness where we cease to take part in, or be subject to, the illusions of pain in this world, and instead live immersed in a state of peace and freedom. But we will only really start to enjoy planet Earth once we reach a state of Truth. This is very much like saying we'll graduate from high school once we complete our senior year. But some people hate high school. From start to finish, they simply cannot wait to graduate and get out. Then there are others that love high school – they join clubs and activities, they enjoy sports and parties and friendships, they create and participate in a community of loving interactions. These people graduate too, but they have a much more beautiful journey, and they make the journey infinitely more meaningful and fun for those around them.

The people who hate high school from start to finish and yet do the work to graduate are much like people who simply want to get enlightened so that they can get away from the lunatics with which planet Earth is populated (and really, who can blame them). The ones who love high school are the people who are trying to achieve a state of Truth, not just graduate. Both graduate, but only one group really enjoyed the journey.

Let us rest assured that we will all reach enlightenment one day, for it is the culmination of our spiritual journey as human beings. That is not something to worry about, and it is not the point of this book. This book is written to help us understand how to transform ourselves so that we can create a state of Heaven on Earth. This is a guidebook for how to change this planet from a giant school that everyone just can't wait to graduate from to a giant slice of heaven that we know we'll miss even as we move on to bigger and better things.

THIRTY-TWO

What Does the Future Hold?

Will there be a "Golden Age?" Yes indeed, there will be, and we are on our way there right now. However, this beautiful age is more appropriately called "The Age of Truth," and to get there, we will first pass through "The Age of Grace and Love."

According to our research, when 35% of the population has an ego under 44% and is therefore in a state of Grace, and has a soulfulness of above 40, which is a state of Love, we will enter the Age of Grace and Love, which is the beginning of the Golden Age. Remember, right now only 5% of the population has an ego score under 45%, and only 5% has a soulfulness score of above 40.

Those numbers might seem discouraging, as though it is a very, very long way to the Age of Grace and Love. Yet this is untrue. What is most amazing is that we are so, so close to being there.

Only the thinnest veil separates us from this beautiful state of humanity. This became apparent to us when we started seeing our clients dropping their egos up to 50 points within three months of active ego dropping. Fifty points is from the high ego zone all the way down to a state of Grace– in a couple of months. Imagine - what if just 30% of the population engaged in such a challenge? That's all it would take. We could be there, as a global human society, in just three months, perhaps less. Yes, there would be maintenance required, but as everyone knows, maintenance is not difficult, any more than remembering to brush our teeth or bathe is difficult.

As you may remember, it takes a little more effort to get to a state of Truth – your ego must be at 35% or below, and your soulfulness must be at 60 or more. Again, we will arrive at the Age of Truth, the height of the Golden Age, if and when 35% of the world's population has achieved a state of Truth.

There is a big difference between the Age of Grace and Love, and the Age of Truth. In the former, global human consciousness will have arrived at a state of Reason and Wisdom. In the latter, global human consciousness will be at the level of Joy. So the beginning of the Golden Age is where we finally enter into a state of sanity as a global human society, which is wonderful – but the height of the Golden Age, the Age of Truth, is when we are not only sane, we are Joyful. This is the global party of Heaven on Earth.

This is where we hope to arrive. Let's not just aim for sanity. That's like just hoping for law and order. Let's set our sights higher and create Heaven right here on Earth. It is possible, but it is not a foregone conclusion. Again, this is the elective path, not the required one. We have to choose it, both as individuals and as a society.

Various religious traditions believe there will be an "end of days" conflict, the result of which will be massive destruction; death to all sinners and the righteous will live in peace for a thousand years. If we examine this belief in light of our research, it sounds like a final group ego conflict that results in the lowering of all egos once and for all through its ferocity. Since the way most human beings are currently choosing to lower their egos is the passive way, it does seem possible that various groups will call to themselves a hugely destructive conflict in order to deal with their own egos once and for all. But is it necessary?

No, of course not. We become passive participants in terrible outside events only because we refuse the path of active ego lowering. If just a small percentage of the population were to take up the challenge of lowering their own egos and expanding their own hearts, such massive group conflicts would be avoided, because they would become unnecessary. They only exist as vehicles for our growth.

It is critical to realize that this concept of active ego lowering and soulfulness building is simple. It is not difficult, nor is it painful. It's much like actively pursuing anything else – perhaps going to the gym is a good example. So many people make the resolution every year to "get in shape," and yet they have a hard time keeping to it. What most of them find is that the hardest thing to do is to simply get themselves to the gym. Once they are there, working out is not only easy; they find they feel much better for doing it.

It's the same with this. The things we need to practice in order to actively lower our egos, or actively build our soulfulness, are not difficult, and we feel so much better, so much lighter, happier and freer when we do. The only challenge we have to overcome is our resistance to change. But really, we've overcome that before, haven't we? If human beings managed to get to the moon – surely we can get over our own egos, can we not? If we have managed to stretch ourselves in every way possible to uncover our own ingenuity, surely we can stretch ourselves to accommodate and express the full potential of the human heart.

IV. The Rulebook

THIRTY-THREE

Conclusion

We had no idea when we began this research where it would lead us. As mentioned at the very beginning of the book, the gratitude we feel for the experiences of our lives, particularly the most difficult ones, is now overwhelming. The only things we mourn now are the times when we didn't have the understanding to see the gift in those difficult trials, and as a result, let our egos go back up through anger, resentment, or bitterness and stored some trauma away to deal with later. Ah, the tragedy of a wasted opportunity!

Guy's life no longer seems so terrible to us. Rather, it is a triumph: in one lifetime, his soul took on the challenge of lowering his ego from 99% to 30% and he achieved it. True, he suffered through it, because like most of us, he was unaware of the true meaning of his experiences and therefore had to go through a lot of pain in order to destroy his ego.

He took the Path of Pain and Suffering and although it worked, the name fit his experience. Yet he won in the end, and we only wish we could know him and watch him grow in his next life.

After having conducted all this research we feel very much like children who were playing a game for years against an unseen opponent who knew all the rules while we understood none of them. Finally we started researching the rules of the game and what a difference it makes to know the rules of the game you are playing! Our whole perspective on the future of humanity on this planet has changed: we now believe it is completely possible for every individual to transform him or herself to live life steeped in a state of Truth, and to support everyone else as they do this, too. Suffering is truly optional. We have the ability and the tools to live lives steeped in Grace, Love, and Truth, and we have discovered that the process of reaching that state is much simpler than we had ever dreamed.

We leave you now with the "Rulebook" as we have uncovered it thus far. We hope you find it helpful as you continue on your journey through the wonderful game of Life.

The RuleBook

1. The object of the game is to lower your ego and raise your soulfulness and to compassionately support everyone else in the game as they do the same.

2. Your ego will try to mire you in self-pity and get you to believe you are a helpless victim of circumstances beyond your control. This is an illusion and will only distract you from achieving the object of rule #1.

3. There are two paths to lower your ego: The Path of Pain and Suffering (the default path) and the Path of Conscious Transformation (the optional path). They are exactly like their names describe them. It is up to you to choose which way to go.

4. Transformation is not optional. Just as you cannot escape gravity, you cannot escape the continual opportunities that Life will give you to grow.

The RuleBook - cont.

5. If you choose the Path of Conscious Transformation, there are specific lists of things you can practice to lower your ego and increase your soulfulness.

6. If you do not make the choice to pursue the Path of Conscious Transformation, you will, by default, be on the Path of Pain and Suffering. This Path also has specific lists of things that will lower your ego, but on this path they will be randomly imposed on you, not chosen by you.

7. The price to pay for traveling the default path is you will have trauma to release even after you arrive in the low ego zone. This takes some time and usually requires outside help from people or therapies designed to do this.

8. One way to release trauma on your own is to simply take full and complete responsibility for every activity and condition in your entire life experience by recognizing that all circumstances in your life reflect your current state of consciousness.

9. If you want to understand world events and phenomena, look at them from the perspective of group ego interaction. Remember that group conflicts are what give us opportunities as individuals for ego crushing and soulfulness building.

10. The way to stop suffering as a result of group ego conflicts is to lower our egos into the low ego zone and then release our identification with any group by holding a place of compassion for all individuals in all groups.

11. Remember that lowering your ego brings you peace, and that building your soulfulness brings you love and fulfillment. Seek both if you want to experience joy, which is defined as a State of Truth.

12. You are immeasurably important, as is every unique individual in this world. It is only through our individual efforts that we will achieve a state of Heaven on Earth as a global human society.

Glossary

1. **Suffering**

   This is an all-encompassing term for any emotional pain suffered.

2. **Loss**

   Loss can include the death of a person close to the individual, loss of a valued object or property or simply the dissolution of a situation or relationship to which the individual was attached.

3. **Failure**

   Failure can mean any sort of failure – failure of a relationship, a business or any sort of venture.

4. **Forgiveness**

   True forgiveness means releasing the anger and pain we associate with any person (including ourselves) as a result of our perception of wrongdoing on that person's part.

5. Non-Defensiveness

Non-defensiveness is the act of releasing our need to defend or prove ourselves to others or to direct blame (or perceived blame) away from ourselves.

6. Non-Judgment & Acceptance

Non-judgment and acceptance are really the same thing. Both mean we accept people and conditions as they are, rather than labeling them either "good" or "bad." When we accept people and conditions as they are, we do not resist them and we are therefore able to engage fully and completely in the present moment.

7. Selfless Service

Selfless service is the act of humbly serving others without expectation of any reward for our actions. Selfless service means that we neither know nor care whether others are aware of our service or thank us for it, and certainly do not advertise or hold others in debt to our service. We serve simply out of gratitude for what we ourselves have been given, that is, the gift of

Life itself, and in the realization that we are all connected in oneness.

8. Gratitude

True gratitude lies in the conscious realization of all we have been given in this life. It is the recognition that none of us "deserves" Life and all its bounties, and that no matter how many negative things or circumstances we may be tempted to give our attention to, there are always more positive things and circumstances available to us if we simply choose to focus upon them instead.

9. Surrender

Surrender is the act of setting aside our own expectations and allowing the universal Life force to act through us, trusting that Its infinite intelligence and love will always bring us to the best and most meaningful outcome possible.

10. Equanimity

True equanimity is a state of complete non-reactivity. In this state, we recognize that any news that comes to us that may appear threatening to our well-being is nothing other than a false suggestion that Life is not working in perfect accord. We therefore do not react in a defensive posture, but rather stay calm and at peace within ourselves, responding according to our highest wisdom.

11. Patience

The practice of patience is a profound one, and it is found in the little moments of life: when we are stopped at a traffic light and the car in front of us does not move immediately when the light turns green, or when we find ourselves in a long line at the DMV, for example. The practice of patience in these cases means we do not try to force these situations or people to conform to our expectations or schedules but instead recognize that our time is infinite, and our lives and schedules will continue to flow despite what seems to be an interruption in our schedule.

12. Renunciation

Renunciation is the act of fully, completely and irrevocably rejecting false beliefs and patterns within ourselves. A good example is an addict who completely quits her addiction.

13. Taking full responsibility

Taking full responsibility means that we consciously realize and acknowledge that all conditions and activities in our life reflect the state of our own consciousness and actions. Nothing is in our life by chance, and we are never innocent victims of circumstance. All conditions and circumstances are not only there by our design (either conscious or unconscious), they are there to support our transformation into the highest and most conscious version of ourselves.

14. Restriction

The practice of restriction means we consciously refrain from engaging in activities or behaviors that support our lower selves, or which encourage us to "check out" of the present moment or indulge in behavior that distracts us from expressing our higher selves. Common compulsions we find our clients need to restrict are such things as surfing the internet, channel-flipping TV watching, gambling, porn, substance abuse of any kind, and self-abuse of any kind such as compulsive worrying, anger, envy, judgment, dwelling in the past, etc.

15. Compassion

Practicing compassion means that not only do we not judge others when we see them in a place of pain, but we also understand their pain from a position of love and empathy.

16. Admission of Wrongdoing & Making Amends

Admission of wrongdoing and making amends is simple: we recognize when we have wronged another by not acting in integrity, we admit this to the injured party, and we do what we can to correct the situation.

17. Humility

True humility means that we do not take credit for our accomplishments but instead recognize that we are simply channels through which the universal Life force acts.

With humility, we know it is our great privilege to be the channel for such wonderful acts.

18. Humiliation

Humiliation is forced humility. If we are not humble, we will be humbled through an experience of shame.

19. Dependency

Dependency means that in one way or another, we find ourselves unable to function independently. This may be due to physical or financial incapacitation; in any event, we find ourselves dependent upon the goodwill of others for our own well-being.

20 . Incapacitation

Incapacitation refers to any condition in which we find ourselves experiencing less than functional health. This could be due to a disease, to a physical disability, or to a mental or emotional condition.

21. Untimely Death

Untimely death refers to either our own untimely death or the untimely death of a loved one.

Appendix A: Individual Egos in History

The following famous people and their ego scores at death are listed here as a reference:

1.	Genghis Khan	100%
2.	Mao Tse-Tung	100%
3.	Francisco Franco	100%
4.	Joseph Stalin	100%
5.	Alexander the Great	100%
6.	Muhammed Atta	100%
7.	David Koresh	100%
8.	Henry VIII	99%
9.	Eva Peron	99%
10.	Martin Luther	97%
11.	Karl Marx	97%
12.	Voltaire	75%
13.	Socrates	60%
14.	Mohandas Gandhi	60%
15.	Abraham Lincoln	60%
16.	John F. Kennedy	60%
17.	Albert Einstein	45%
18.	Joan of Arc	20%
19.	Moses	0%
20.	Rabbi Shimon bar Yochai	0%
21.	Jesus of Nazareth	0%

Appendix B: Famous Figures and Organizations of Soulfulness in History

The following famous figures and organizations and their soulfulness scores are listed here as a reference:

1.	Mary, Mother of Jesus	95%
2.	Mother Theresa	70%
3.	Pope John XXIII	60%
4.	Bill W. (Watson)	60%
5.	Mary Baker Eddy	60%
6.	Doctors Without Borders	60%
7.	Mohandas Gandhi	60%
8.	Padre Pio	60%
9.	Ralph Waldo Emerson	60%
10.	Ashoka the Great	60%
11.	William Wilberforce	60%
12.	Corrie ten Boom	60%
13.	Billy Graham	60%
14.	Emily Green Balch	50%
15.	Louis Armstrong	50%
16.	Mark Twain	50%
17.	Jim Henson	50%
18.	Bob Marley	50%
19.	Morrie Schwartz	50%
20.	Richard Pryor	50%
21.	Ronald Reagan	40%

Appendix C: Trauma Release Techniques

The following are two of the many techniques that we use in our practice to help our clients release past trauma.

1. *Brain State Conditioning™*
Brain State Conditioning™ is a highly sophisticated form of neurofeedback. It works to erase trauma imprints from the nervous system by helping the brain build new, balanced neuro-pathways. This is a highly efficient technique and most people notice remarkable changes within the first three days of practice. For more information, read Lee Gerdes' excellent book, *Limitless You*, or go to www.yogimind.com.

2. *Trauma Releasing Exercises*
Trauma Releasing Exercises (TRE), were designed to address the specific need for somatic based trauma recovery therapy. They consist of a series of simple physical exercises designed to produce mild neurogenic tremors in the body. The result is that by allying the client with the body's natural psychogenic tremor response and reinforcing it externally rather than suppressing it and treating

it as pathology, the neuro-physiological and neuro-anatomical homeostasis of the individual is restored. Once this homeostasis is restored, there is both a reported and measurable reduction of psycho-somatic symptoms of PTSD. Please see Dr. David Bercelli's wonderful book, *The Revolutionary Trauma Release Process: Transcend Your Toughest Times*, for more information.

Ego Clearing

1. Equanimity (non-reactivity)

2. Restriction

3. Forgiveness

4. Patience

5. Taking Full Responsibility

6. Humility

7. Surrender

Ego Rising

1.   Lack of discipline

2.   Lack of love

3.   Ingratitude

4.   Feeling of Superiority

5.   Desire for Power and Dominance

6.   Anger and Resentment

7.   Substance Abuse and Addiction

Active Ego Lowering Practices

1. Forgiveness
2. Non-Defensiveness
3. Non-Judgment & Acceptance
4. Selfless Service
5. Gratitude
6. Surrender
7. Equanimity
8. Patience
9. Renunciation
10. Taking full responsibility
11. Restriction
12. Compassion
13. Admission of Wrongdoing & Making Amends
14. Humility

To Build Soulfulness

1. Build community
   (connect with others in a consistent fashion)

2. Support others
   (emotional support and guidance or mentorship)

3. Practice non-defensiveness

4. Educate and learn with others

5. Honor others

6. Cooperate with others

7. Share with others
   (specifically time and money)

8. Provide for others
   (assistance and material needs)

9. Feed others
   (yes, this is its own category, and yes, it is
   that simple)

10. Play with others
    (games, sports activities, general silliness and
    diversion)

11. Celebrate with others
    (join in celebrations or throw them yourself)

12. Share physical affection with others
    (hugs, holding hands, pats on the back)

13. Practice Gratitude

14. Love others

Index of Lists

About the Authors

Brandy Bennitt and Ian Mussman split their time between their home and practice in Santa Barbara and their practice in Los Angeles.

Ian is a Naturopathic Doctor who has practiced for the past 17 years in Los Angeles and Santa Barbara. He uses Biofeedback Resonance Testing to assess his patients. Brandy and her aunt, Loren Bennitt, together own YogiMind, a company that works with Brain State Conditioning™ to erase traumatic imprints from the nervous system and help individuals recover balance and harmony in their lives. She and Ian work closely together, utilizing their complimentary skills and tools to assist their clients achieve vibrant states of emotional and physical health. They are joined in this endeavor by other holistic health care practitioners at Health Within Wellness Center in Los Angeles.

The pair are currently working on their next book, and can be reached for appointments through their website at www.yogimind.com.

Made in the USA
Las Vegas, NV
25 February 2021